Television Storyworlds as Virtual Space

Television Storyworlds as Virtual Space

M. King Adkins

LEXINGTON BOOKS
Lanham • Boulder • New York • London

Published by Lexington Books
An imprint of The Rowman & Littlefield Publishing Group, Inc.
4501 Forbes Boulevard, Suite 200, Lanham, Maryland 20706
www.rowman.com

Unit A, Whitacre Mews, 26-34 Stannary Street, London SE11 4AB

British Library Cataloguing in Publication Information Available

Library of Congress Cataloging-in-Publication Data

Library of Congress Cataloging-in-Publication Data

Names: Adkins, M. King, author.
Title: Television storyworlds as virtual space / M. King Adkins.
Description: Lanham : Lexington Books, [2018] | Includes bibliographical references and index.
Identifiers: LCCN 2018022629 (print) | LCCN 2018029298 (ebook) | ISBN 9781498529617 (electronic) | ISBN 9781498529600 (cloth : alk. paper)
Subjects: LCSH: Television—Philosophy. | Television programs—Social aspects. | Virtual reality—Social aspects. | Postmodernism—Social aspects.
Classification: LCC PN1992.55 (ebook) | LCC PN1992.55 .A35 2018 (print) | DDC 302.234/5—dc23
LC record available at https://lccn.loc.gov/2018022629

™ The paper used in this publication meets the minimum requirements of American National Standard for Information Sciences—Permanence of Paper for Printed Library Materials, ANSI/NISO Z39.48-1992.

Printed in the United States of America

For Wren Costello Adkins

Contents

Acknowledgments

Acknowledgment sections generally thank people for offering their insight and advice, or perhaps for doing supplementary research, or providing financial support. More important to me, though, as I have worked on this book has been the psychological and emotional support, the freedom and space in which to work, and the encouragement to keep going when I felt hopelessly overwhelmed. Many of the people I thank here are professional colleagues, but I consider them all to be my friends and family. I appreciate what they do more than they can possibly know. They include,

John and Adriane Dreyer
Christy Tidwell and Neil Robinson
Kayla and Jason Pritchard
Frank and Janet Van Nuys
Ida Bostian and Brad Blackmon

I want especially to highlight Joseph Lundquist, who cares just as deeply as I do about popular culture and understanding how it works, and who—because he possesses a scientist's mind—always helps remind me to consider viewpoints other than the humanist's.

I would like to thank the South Dakota School of Mines and Technology's Devereaux Library, especially Josh Wilkinson and the ILL department, for working with me to ensure I had access to the resources I needed.

Additionally, I must thank my family—my wife, Katie; my daughters, Samantha and Wren; my parents Sam Adkins, Vicky Adkins, and Jackie Campbell—who put up with a lot from me and without whom I simply couldn't write.

Finally, I offer thanks to the many television artists—the writers, directors, producers, actors, and crew members—who have given us all more than seventy years' worth of amazing worlds to explore. I talk at length in this book about contemporary television and its storytelling power, but that is not to undercut all the important work done from television's inception by gifted artists, to better understand their chosen medium and to prepare the ground upon which its more recent glories have been built. Whatever my junior high school teachers may have tried to convince me about TV's failings, my own life is infinitely richer because of television.

Introduction

TV, A Vast . . . Land

Television scholars have never forgotten FCC chairman Newton Minnow's 1961 description of TV as "a vast wasteland" (2003). His choice of phrase could not have been more withering. Jonathan Gray and Amanda Lotz, in their recent historical survey of TV scholarship—*TV Studies*—call it "Arguably the most famous statement about television to this day" (2012, 11). And while these days television needs no defense as an artistic medium, for those of us passionate about the form Minnow's words still sting. Many of us remain singularly driven in our careers by a simple desire to prove him wrong.

To be fair, I should put Minnow's comment in context. He had only just praised TV three sentences before: "When television is good, nothing—not the theater, not the magazines or newspapers—nothing is better" (398). Television, the medium, was not the problem; his target was "inferior" programming. Even on this score, though, he was wrong: the 1960–1961 primetime TV schedule included such classics as *Walt Disney Presents*, *Maverick*, *The Ed Sullivan Show*, *Perry Mason*, *Gunsmoke*, *The Andy Griffith Show*, *Alfred Hitchcock Presents*, *Father Knows Best*, *The Adventures of Ozzie and Harriet*, *Wagon Train*, *My Three Sons*, *Rawhide*, *Route 66*, *The Twilight Zone*, *Leave It to Beaver*, *Have Gun—Will Travel*, *The Danny Thomas Show*, *The Jack Benny Program*, *The Bugs Bunny Show*, and *The Flintstones*. Minnow described these shows as full of "mayhem, violence, sadism, murder, Western bad men, Western good men, private eyes, gangsters, more violence, and cartoons" (398). Perhaps; but none of them lacked for "imagination" "creativity" or "experimentation" as he also insisted.

As wrong as Minnow may have been though, in making his point he struck upon a fascinating metaphor, one I have borrowed as the central metaphor of this book: TV as landscape. In fact, television can usefully be thought of in terms of space, as a "world" or rather many worlds—a whole host of virtual spaces viewers enter, explore, inhabit week after week, episode after episode. This book is about TV's capacity to create and sustain such spaces. In the following pages, I offer a framework for thinking about TV's importance as a medium and try to explore some of its more salient features. But as an added bonus, I take some satisfaction in using Minnow's own metaphor against him.

THE SPACE OF THIS BOOK

I have organized this book into roughly three parts.

The first of these—which includes chapters 1–3—lays the theoretical groundwork for my argument. I begin chapter 1 with what I regard as an essential question, a question that hangs over the entire book: what happens to us when we encounter a television narrative, or for that matter any sort of narrative? We know from experience that we can be drawn into stories, that we can sometimes invest in them as though they were almost "real." Narratology has developed the precise term "storyworld" to help explain how this happens: a storyworld is a sort of alternative space into which we project ourselves mentally, a space we "experience," at least on some psychological and emotional levels. But this idea—of an alternate, imaginative space, dates back much farther than narratology, to what are apparently the roots of Western art itself. At the same time, this idea is encoded into the very contemporary, almost futuristic concept of virtual reality. In fact, as Marie-Laure Ryan conceives of this term, we might almost regard it as synonymous with storyworld. Finally, though, I argue that—while the storyworld may—and most often does—include characters and events, its most important aspect is its worldliness. That is, for a storyworld to truly draw us in, it must offer a space for us to inhabit.

Having established the concept of storyworlds and virtual reality, as well as their relationship to one another, in chapter 2 I turn specifically to television, and how its particular characteristics as a medium make it especially suited to generating full, complex virtual spaces. Television draws, of course, on the history of narrative in Western culture, and I begin by connecting it to that history. However, my true goal in this chapter is to distinguish television from other media forms. In particular, I focus on television's immediacy, its domesticity, and its seriality as among its defining elements. Together, these three give television narratives a unique flavor, one that is especially suited to generating inhabitable spaces, but that is also suited to growing those spaces over time.

Finally, in chapter 3, I focus in on some very specific techniques television series use to accomplish these tasks. I begin with a basic look at visuals and movement and particularly how these two often work in tandem to give viewers an experience of space that has both depth and breadth. As the chapter continues, I move on to consider some of the more complex ways in which television—especially contemporary television—has developed its spaces not just through specific techniques but by reference to a number of specific themes and motifs. This chapter gives lots of concrete examples designed to set up the next section of the book, which delves more deeply into more specialized topics.

This second section of the book corresponds roughly to chapters 4–7. Within these chapters I am primarily interested in applying the theory I have set up to investigating a series of televisual topics. In chapter 4, for example, I focus on series' opening credit sequences and especially how they repeatedly move us smoothly back into the world of a series. I offer a number of concrete examples, which help me to establish some key television genres that I then explore over the course of the next three chapters.

One reason I begin with the subject of opening credits is that it allows me to think about the nature of television beginnings. In chapter 5, I turn to another sort of television beginning—children's programming. My interest here is in showing another way television starts for us—as children encountering our first series. Kids TV, as I point out here, is not merely about teaching us how to count, or the letters of the alphabet. One of its primary functions is to teach us how to interact with the television itself. As a result, many children's shows are hyper-aware of the space they are creating, because it matters how children first experience these spaces, and it matters how they learn to navigate and control them.

In chapter 6 I am concerned with science fiction and particularly post-apocalyptic narratives. Here again, I argue that such narratives offer unique opportunities to think about beginnings and importantly how narratives begin. These genres, by their very nature, take us into a space we do not know and ask us to grapple with that space, figure out how it works, explore it, and push against its boundaries—in short we participate in building such worlds. Thus if we want to understand how a television series creates its spaces, such series offer the perfect laboratory for thinking through the process.

Chapter 7 works in a similar fashion to chapter 6, by focusing on a common television genre, in this case the police drama. Here again, I suggest that the genre is in itself a strong fit for television because of space's centrality. Mysteries are about uncovering, discovering: what took place here? How did it happen? Who was involved? All of these questions force us to push more deeply into the spaces we encounter, to dig into them and understand them intimately. My central focus in this chapter is on the HBO series *The Wire*, a series that took the basic building blocks of the traditional police drama and used them to lay the city of Baltimore completely bare.

Finally, in my last two chapters, I turn again to theory, though with a different purpose in mind than I have in my first section. Here I want to think in a broad sense about how television interacts with the world and beyond this what its future might be. In chapter 8 I draw on postmodern theory to argue that television in particular has done a great deal to undermine our sense of "reality," to blur the lines between the real and artificial. So effective has it been, that it might be argued television, not digital, computer-based VR, is actually the true "virtual reality." Through its very mechanisms it turned all of reality into one giant simulation.

This then leads me to my final chapter where I consider television's future as a medium. While TV itself seems to feel a great deal of anxiety about being usurped by new technologies, I argue that its fears are misplaced, that perhaps the forms through which we watch television may change, but the essential elements that television established—open-ended plot lines that encourage us to enter the narrative space and grow with it—will long endure no matter what technological form we may access them in.

Hopefully, in addition to seeing the book as three sections, you will also find a number of themes that weave their way through the book. While I am not necessarily trying to create a television history, for example, I do offer some thoughts on television's past in comparison to its contemporary state. My thoughts on postmodernism are summarized in chapter 8, but they are likewise scattered throughout this chapter and others, from my discussion of *Teletubbies* in chapter 5 to my examination of *The Wire* in chapter 7. And while I focus on television "endings" in the final chapter of the book, hopefully these are of a piece with the beginnings I deal with in other spots.

Finally, television is a "vast" subject. Whole books have been written about single networks like MTV, or even single shows like *The Big Bang Theory*. Given this fact, I cannot hope to say all there is to say on the subject; nor can I present any argument here that would be completely unassailable. Instead, let me admit up front that I offer only one perspective on television as a medium, one I think helps to understand a great deal of what television does, but certainly not all.

I also want to set some limitations to my study at the outset. First, my primary interest here is in narrative discourse, and in the main, series television. I talk in spots about reality TV, and sports and news programming are implicit in many of my arguments. Most of my examples, however, are drawn from series that might best be described as telling fictional stories.

Throughout the book I frequently treat sitcoms, dramas, and other genres in essentially the same ways. Likewise I don't take the time to discuss the fine differences between shows that appear on networks such as ABC or FOX and those that appear on pay networks like HBO or subscription services such as Netflix. I probably don't talk enough about the differences in American and

British television. I do recognize the many and important differences among these kinds of programming and the fact that presentation necessarily shapes content, but spending too much time here on such topics would take me away from my central objective, a more generalized argument about the nature of television as a medium.

Chapter 1

"Where Everybody Knows Your Name"

TV Worlds

Each episode of *Cheers* begins with the same lines sung over simple piano, lines that suggest "the world"—what we might for the sake of simplicity call the "real" world—can be tough, so tough in fact that "sometimes" you just want to "get away" from it. Within the context of the series, the bar Cheers fulfills that need; it is a place to escape to, a refuge, a welcoming place, "where everybody knows your name." Of course, the series' theme song isn't suggesting that Norm, Cliff, and Frasier literally step outside the real world and into another like Captain James T. Kirk energizing down to an unexplored planet. Despite the phrasing, "world" here doesn't mean "*the* world," but something more akin to "the rest of the world," or "the working world," or perhaps, to borrow a phrase, "the rat race."

The song works on another level as well, though: it beckons characters to the bar, but it beckons us as viewers into the world of the show. The show *Cheers* is also a "place" where we as viewers can "get away." For eleven years, from 1982 to 1993, we could tune in each week, leave our "world" behind for half an hour, and "get away" to a completely other world (these days we can go there any time we want using whatever streaming service might currently be playing the series). In this sense, the bar truly is an "other" world, one that exists outside our own reality, one to which we relocate every time we watch.

April 2017 saw the conclusion of the A&E television series, *Bates Motel*. In the wrap-up documentary to the series, *Bates Motel: the Checkout* (2017), cast, crew, and fans share their feelings about the show's success. Over and over again the actors mention how much they will miss the characters they played and the spaces those characters inhabited. Freddie Highmore, who played central character Norman Bates, seems especially attached to his experience: "I feel like this isn't really goodbye. There's got to be more,

more somewhere. I don't think I'm willing to say goodbye yet." Meanwhile, fans in the documentary talk about their love/hate relationship with Norman, show off their series-inspired artwork, and admit to crying during specific scenes. It makes sense then that one word that continues to come up in the documentary is "world." Highmore uses it; so does Kerry Ehrin, one of the show's creators: "We all had a vision that the show would have a humanity to it—humor—that it would weirdly be a fun *world* to hang out in" (emphasis added). But what does it mean for us to become so involved with a TV show? What does it say that both those who make these shows and those who watch them think about them not merely as entertainments, or stories, but as "worlds"?

In fact, the word "world" gets applied to television series with some regularity. Some of these uses seem obvious, such as those related to science fiction—David Gerrold's *The World of Star Trek* (1973) for example, or the 1976 promotional book *The World of Doctor Who*. After all, science fiction often introduces us to new worlds—even new galaxies—in a quite literal sense. But over the past fifty years "world" has increasingly shown up in relation to all sorts of television programming. "The World of *Preacher* Is a Violent Place," proclaims an article on SyFyWire.com (Moore 2016). "The world of *Justified* [. . .] is full of messy, complicated, and great female characters," Morgan Glennon writes in a review for the *Huffington Post* (2013). In an interview with series creator David Chase, James Hibberd refers to "the world of *The Sopranos*" (2017). In an article for Vulture.com about the real-life serial killer Edmund Kemper, Brian Tallerico writes of the "world of *Mindhunter*" (2017), while, writing for Forbes.com, Dani Di Placido calls the same show "David Fincher's grimy, green-stained world" (2017). In an article for *The New Yorker* in 2012, Patrick Radden Keefe notes, "One of the chief delights, for me anyway, of the high-end cable drama is the opportunity to become enveloped in a lushly conjured world with its own history, geography, and social codes." Keefe goes on to suggest just what "world" might mean in many of these contexts: "over years of watching, [such worlds] can begin to seem not just plausible, but real."

Nor is the use of the term limited to pop culture fan sites, as evidenced by books like *Buffy, Ballads, and Bad Guys Who Sing: Music in the Worlds of Joss Whedon* (Leonard 2010); *The Television World of Pushing Daisies* (Burger 2011); and *The Inner World of Doctor Who: Psychoanalytic Reflections in Time and Space* (MacRury and Rustin 2013). Jason Mittell, one of today's most prominent television scholars, refers to *The Wire* in a recent essay as "a vast world." Michael James Intintoli's decidedly academic *Taking Soaps Seriously: The World of Guiding Light* (1984) appeared almost forty-five years ago; the equally academic *You Win or You Die: The Ancient World of Game of Thrones* (Lushkov 2017) appeared just six months ago.

In most of these cases, "world" seems to suggest a kind of alternate reality, an "other" space we can inhabit. While we may ultimately recognize these spaces as separate and independent from the real world, we frequently invest in them as though they contain some measure of reality. As Keefe notes above, we can come to regard them as "real" at least in some senses. For example, no matter how fictional their "characters" might be, we may react to those characters in real emotional and even physical ways: we might experience anxiety when a character is being hunted by the police, or cry like those fans of *Bates Motel* when a character we've become attached to dies.

In early 2018, *Major Crimes* ended its six year run on the TNT network. The show was a popular spinoff that followed closely on the heels of TNT's Kyra Sedgewick-vehicle, *The Closer*, and that incorporated many of the earlier show's characters. After thirteen years, fans of the franchise were understandably disappointed to see these characters go. But this disappointment turned to rage when producers decided to "kill off" *Major Crimes*' central character, Captain Sharon Raydor, a full four episodes before the series finale. Adding insult to injury in many viewers' minds, Raydor wasn't killed in the line of duty, pursuing justice for some grieving family. Instead, she passed away unexpectedly from heart disease. Fans wanted her to live on, but barring that they wanted a narratively satisfying ending for her. Though creator James Duff defended his decision saying, "we wanted to give viewers a chance to mourn with us as we fade to black" (Canfield 2018), fans staged a protest of sorts online by changing their social profile pictures to a shot of actress Mary McDonnell's name from the series credits. McDonnell herself endorsed the protest, noting, "losing her, I think, felt like a kick in the solar plexus to a lot of amazing men and women out there" (2018). The fact that a fictional event involving fictional characters can not only stir physical reactions but lead viewers to respond with protests argues that such worlds maintain at least some measure of reality.

A HISTORY OF STORYWORLDS

An entire branch of philosophy and logic—possible worlds theory—has developed around explaining our relationships to fictional worlds from an ontological perspective. Relying on formal semantics, possible worlds theory seeks a structure for considering all the potential ways we might think about our world and the system of satellite worlds that exist around it (Ryan 2005). Everyday reality is defined as "The Actual World" (TAW). Other "worlds" might arise as the result of storytelling, dreams, predictions, even linguistic devices such as metaphors. Each takes us imaginatively to a place outside our own everyday lived reality. The resulting systems can be quite complex, as when a character in a fictional story tells a story about a dream he had the day before, or a fictional character participates in a historical event and interacts with a "real" historical figure. Such instances can require complicated equations to sort out what's happening. In "Truth in Fiction," for example, David Lewis writes of Sherlock Holmes and his possible cocaine use: "A sentence of the form 'In the fiction f, p' is nonvacuously true iff [if and only if] some world where f is told as known fact and p is true differs less from our actual world, on balance, than does any world where f is told as known fact and p is not true" (1978, 42). While formulas like these can help untangle our levels of thinking, they leave little room for discussion of the *experience* of the text; in the end, they don't answer the question of why our body jumps when a zombie's face appears unexpectedly on screen, or why we tense up during a car chase.

Somewhat more practical is the use to which recent narratology has put possible worlds theory. David Herman, for instance, has called for reassessing the relation between narrative theory, linguistics, and structuralism so that it explains our experience of other worlds in more concrete terms. In *Story Logic,* Herman writes, "To my mind, both narrative theory and language theory should [. . .] be viewed as resources for—elements of—the broader endeavor of cognitive science. The result: a jointly narratological and linguistic approach to stories construed as strategies for building mental models of the world" (2004, 2). Herman's work remains grounded in linguistics, but his statements open the door to thinking about artistic worlds as mental projections, projections produced by words and narrative structures to be sure, but very much experienced by those who encounter them. Herman and other narratologists use the word "storyworlds" in reference to such projections, a term Herman defines as "mental models of who did what to and with whom, when, where, and why, and in what fashion in the world to which recipients [readers] relocate" (2004, 5).

Richard Gerrig, pushing further into the cognitive effects of storyworlds, describes that "relocation" process in even more emotional terms: "Readers become 'lost in a book'; moviegoers are surprised when the lights come back up; television viewers care desperately about the fates of soap opera characters; museum visitors are captivated by the stories encoded in daubs of paint. In each case, a narrative serves to transport an experiencer away from the here and now" (1999, 3). This description seems to capture precisely the kind of experience those creators and fans of *Bates Motel* insist the show provides, the kind of outrage Sharon Raydor's death elicited. And those of us who never miss an episode of *Game of Thrones*, or *Breaking Bad*, or *General Hospital*, who binge watch new seasons of *Orange Is the New Black* the day Netflix releases them, recognize what Gerrig says as well. We feel like we know Jim Rockford, or Tony Soprano, or Emma Swan. We get caught up emotionally in their struggles: we cry during *M*A*S*H*'s final moments, as Hawkeye rises in the helicopter and sees BJ's "Goodbye" message written in stones on the ground; we nod in smug satisfaction when *Law and Order*'s prosecutor, Jack McCoy, breaks a cynical CEO on the stand; we get caught up in Mary Richards's complicated feelings of grief, hilarity, and guilt at Chuckles the Clown's funeral. Again, this isn't to suggest we don't recognize these moments as "fiction." We know how to step back and see them with objectivity, as "merely" television. Nevertheless, their ability to impact us in such direct ways argues that we "know" these characters and events no less than we know our friends and family, the places, and the events that populate our day-to-day lives.

While contemporary narratology offers a useful language for thinking about how we experience television "worlds," the concept of storyworlds and the fascination with how they affect us is not new. Some 2,500 years ago, Western art's first theorist, Plato, understood art in very similar terms and, in fact, fretted over its ability to "transport" us away from the here and now. His "Allegory of the Cave" (1968 514a–520a) posits two distinct levels of reality—the one most of us experience in our day-to-day lives, and a deeper, more fundamental reality—the logos of ideal forms that underpins that everyday world. In his famous description of that cave, most of us spend our lives chained, facing the cave wall, while objects are shown behind us casting dim shadows against that wall, shadows we often unwittingly mistake for reality. In such a cosmological system, we have enough trouble seeing the bedrock truth of our existence. Art, an artificial rendering of an artificial shadow, only moves us further away from that truth. Art is "third from what is"—a copy of a copy. In one passage Plato illustrates the central problem by imagining a couch: "There turn out, then, to be these three kinds of couches: one that *is* in nature, which we would say, I suppose, a god produced [. . .] and then one that the carpenter produced [. . .] and one that the painter produced" (595a–598a). The carpenter-produced version, while maintaining a physical existence, remains only a copy of the logos, the ideal form of the couch. The painting then is merely an imitation of an imitation, a "phantom," especially dangerous because it might deceive the "innocent" into accepting it as "real."

And if a painting conjures up a phantom object, fictional narrative—a storyworld—can conjure up entire realms, full of characters and events with whom we may—at our peril—become emotionally—and hence real-ly involved. In fact, Plato banishes Homer and Aeschylus from the utopia he imagines in *The Republic*:

> When even the best of us hear Homer or any other of the tragic poets imitating one of the heroes in mourning and making quite an extended speech with

> lamentation, or, if you like, singing and beating his breast, you know that we enjoy it and that we give ourselves over to following the imitation; suffering along with the hero in all seriousness, we praise as a good poet the man who most puts us in this state. (605a)

Such instances don't simply trick our physical sense of sight; they confuse our experience of reality, offering a fantasy reality in its place, a fantasy in which we might become permanently lost.

Plato's student, Aristotle, begins from a similar premise—art as existing at one move from reality. However, ultimately he praises art for the very same reasons Plato suspects it. In *Poetics* he suggests that "Imitation comes naturally to human beings from childhood (and in this they differ from other animals, i.e. in having a strong propensity for imitation and in learning their earliest lessons through imitation); so does the universal pleasure in imitation" (1996, 3.1.6). But if we are naturally predisposed to imitate, we can also take pleasure in, and even learn from, such imitation: "This is the reason why people take delight in seeing images; what happens is that as they view them they come to understand and work out what each thing is" (3.1.6). Here art's "virtual" character makes it a tool, a simulation that serves as a practice space for living, where we may test out experience without fear of consequences.

From these two thinkers spring the apparently never-ending discussion over art's value versus its dangers. Of Don Quixote, Cervantes writes, "he so immersed himself in those romances that he spent whole days and nights over his books; and thus with little sleeping and much reading, his brains dried up to such a degree that he lost the use of his reason" (2005, Book 1: Part 1). In a similar way Flaubert's Emma Bovary uses, or rather misuses, the imaginary worlds of her novels as an escape from reality: "she read Balzac and George Sand, seeking in them imaginary satisfaction for her own desires" (1904, 36). As new narrative technologies arise, each faces the same criticism. Huxley has his hero, John Savage, reject the "feely"—a version of the cinema featuring sensory effects—and its offer of a reconstructed reality outright: "But I don't want comfort. I want God, I want poetry, I want real danger, I want freedom, I want goodness. I want sin" (2004, 215). A 2007 *South Park* episode ridicules the video game *Guitar Hero* in terms that are strikingly Platonic ("Guitar Queer-O"). In one scene a café full of people begin to clap in time to the rhythmic clicks of a plastic game controller as though they were actually listening to music. One patron exclaims, "Oh, I love this song." Such criticisms can even come couched as dire warnings as in the American Academy of Pediatrics guidelines for screen time, which caution that "too much media use can mean that children don't have enough time during the day to play, study, talk, or sleep" ("American Academy of Pediatrics Announces . . . " 2016).

Yet few today would argue that reading is a dangerous activity as Cervantes does. In the quote above, Huxley holds reading up in opposition to the feely, as the "real" source of feeling—"danger," "freedom," "goodness," "sin." And while newer media including film, television, and video games are still regularly singled out for criticism especially, and ironically, by the mainstream press, most media scholars view these artistic forms in positive terms. If video games, for instance, are liable to misuse, they also hold out the potential for powerful cultural and social change. In *Reality Is Broken*, for example, Jane McGonigal argues that video game simulations might actually hold the solution to many of the world's most pressing problems, from getting our kids to do chores around the house to reversing global climate change (2011).

What matters more than the two poles of this debate though are the similar premises from which they begin. Both recognize art is mimetic. In fact, mimetic doesn't seem quite strong enough a word for what Plato and Aristotle have in mind. Mimesis, after all, implies imitation, accurate in a literal sense, but distinct from the kind of realistic experience these thinkers and their heirs seem to envision. In this version of art history, art offers something more than imitation: it offers an artificial space in which to exist—so real that we might actually mistake it for reality.[1]

And, in fact, the most cutting edge science suggests that, in a certain sense, this is indeed what happens when we experience a storyworld. In a groundbreaking 2009 neurological study, Speer, Reynolds, Swallow, and Zacks had subjects read narratives and monitored their brain activity as they did so. Their conclusions:

> That readers dynamically activate specific visual, motor, and conceptual features of activities while reading about analogous changes in activities in the context of the narrative. Regions involved in processing goal-directed human activity, navigating spatial environments, and manually manipulating objects in the real world increased in activity at points when these specific aspects of the narrated situation were changing. (2009, 995–996)

In other words our brains respond to narrated events, spatial directions, and object descriptions as though they are actual events, directions, and objects. Our brains experience the two classes—real and imagined—in the same way, making one, neurologically anyway, just as real as the other.

The work of Speer and her colleagues is further supported by the earlier 1992 discovery of "mirror neurons," a "neurobiological mechanism by which we understand the actions of others and match observed actions with motor representations of those actions" (Marr 2015, 242). Further research into such neurons has revealed they are primarily responsible for our responses to works of art and explain "why viewers automatically simulate a work's actions and intentions, emotional expressions, and implied movements, including those suggested by brush marks and paint drips—the 'physical traces' of the artist's 'creative actions'" (Marr 2015, 243). What our eyes see we literally experience, whether or not we actually participate in the spectacle. What we encounter, whether it be an actual lion on an African savannah, a framed oil painting of a lion hanging in a gallery, or a lion roaring at us from our television screens, generates the same basic neurological effects.

How does all of this science and theory translate into our experience of *Game of Thrones*, or *Gilmore Girls*, or *Buffy*? One answer to this question involves recognizing that television, in one form or another, has always been with us. In other words, what Plato and Aristotle had to say about Homer might just as well be applied to television. A number of scholars have drawn parallels between mankind's earliest known art form—cave painting—and the moving image. Sean Cubitt describes such images—not crude stylized symbols but sophisticated, realistic drawings of bison, lions, horses—as a kind of proto-cinema: "Before it was technological," he writes, "before history began, there were firelight and shadows, gestures of the shaman, strides of the dancer, puppetry of hand shadows cast on the walls at the rough dawn of consciousness" (2005, 5). Cubitt suggests an ancient art full of movement, where images move—a whole world to inhabit as opposed to mere pictures on a wall.

In his film about the cave drawings discovered near Chauvet, France—*Cave of Forgotten Dreams*—Werner Herzog actually does what Cubbit only imagines—shine his camera lights on these images, noting, "For these Paleolithic painters, the play of light and shadows from their torches could possibly have looked something like this [. . .]. For them, the animals appeared moving, living" (2011). Later, Herzog points out a circular gathering of animals drawn around a small hole in one cave wall, a hole that would at some earlier time have produced a basin of water. The artist has placed these animals together, in imagination, around a lake. He has left an art instillation—a space to be walked through and experienced. It turns out, then, that questions about our responses to television series connect us to the very dawn of our existence.

They also relate to our future. Cubitt relates these images to cinema, but we might also regard them as a kind of primitive "virtual reality." Like Cubitt and Herzog, Howard Rheingold highlights the real-ness of these paintings, noting that they were " 'anamorphic,' painted in a precisely distorted manner on natural protuberances and depressions in the limestone in order to give the rendering a three dimensional appearance when viewed from the proper light and angle" (1992, 381). Drawing on the work of John Pfeiffer, Rheingold goes further, writing, "The earliest virtual realities on earth were constructed laboriously, by lamplight, deep underground" (379–380), and calling these painters "the first technologists" (380).

In fact, virtual reality (VR) offers a useful pivot point for this discussion of "worlds," in that it provides a single description of what art generally, and television in particular, tries to accomplish. The *Oxford English Dictionary* highlights the computer aspect of virtual reality in its definition: "A computer-generated simulation of a lifelike environment that can be interacted with in a seemingly real or physical way by a person." Yet Marie-Laure Ryan argues in *Narrative as Virtual Reality*, that VR represents the ideal for all artistic experience (at least those experiences that spring from a realist impulse). She is careful to maintain that nothing like the dream of VR has yet come to fruition. Even so, that dream lies behind the creative imagination, and "we can use the *idea* of VR as a metaphor for the fullest artistic experience, since in the Platonic world of ideas VR scores a double ten" (2015, 12).

Ryan draws an important analogy. First she argues, "the experience of being inside a computer-generated world involves three distinct components: a sense of being surrounded, a sense of depth, and the possession of a roving point of view." Then crucially, she goes on to point out, "Each of these dimensions improves on, or remediates, a variety of earlier technologies" (39). Ryan's interest is primarily in written texts, but her argument applies equally well to television texts. VR in these terms isn't a singular new technology. Indeed, the conclusion to her work *Narrative as Virtual Reality* suggests that true VR may not even be possible. Rather each artistic technology, from cave paintings, to novels, to film, to television, should be viewed in terms of how it best works to capture the VR ideal.

STORYWORLD SPACES

Like Ryan, I want to use virtual reality as a metaphor, in this case for looking specifically at television, one of the technologies that seems almost to prefigure VR. This book considers just what television offers or contributes as a medium toward the dream of "true VR." In fact, one reason why VR offers such a useful metaphor for television, in particular, is because of its emphasis on space, for I will argue that a sense of an imaginative space is at the heart of what television offers, or at least it is among the most important aspects of the television experience.

Ryan's work pushes narratology beyond even a cognitive framework for thinking about the storyworld. She seeks what she terms a "phenomenology of reading, or more broadly, experiencing art" (1) a "sense of 'presence' through which the user feels corporally connected to the virtual world" (8). This phenomenology, while it may involve elements of story and instances of character, ultimately comes down to a sense of place. In fact, as she points out, many instances of VR don't involve a narrative as such at all. Rather, like *USAToday*'s recent foray into the medium, VR more often simply provides an opportunity to participate in an experience—crossing the Mexican border through a series of dark tunnels, zip lining through a jungle forest, or riding a roller coaster. Though these experiences often involve action, they typically don't include a "plot" in the classical sense of the term.

Ryan traces this idea of a "plural text" that "cannot take narrative form" to Roland Barthes and his dream of "a text that renews itself constantly and holds the reader forever fascinated—which means forever captive—in stark contrast to the consumerist page-turners that we read for the plot, driven by the desire to find out how it ends" (191). She holds up as examples the online virtual experience *Second Life*, and *Placeholder*, a VR drama project that involved "multi-person narrative action in virtual environments." In Ryan's description, *Placeholder*'s "openly stated purpose is to create a sense of place, and its architecture is more indebted to a poetics of space than to a poetics of plot" (232).

David Herman and Richard Gerrig likewise focus on place and space as the most important aspect of the storyworld experience. Gerrig's description, above, includes crucially the phrase "a narrative serves to transport an experiencer away from the here and now." Gerrig goes further in his definition of a storyworld as, "a space one experiences, if only psychologically:

1. Someone ('the traveler') is transported
2. By some means of transportation
3. As a result of performing certain actions.
4. The traveler goes some distance from his or her world of origin,
5. Which makes some aspects of the world of origin inaccessible.
6. The traveler returns to the world of origin, somewhat changed by the journey." (1999, 10–11)

The repeated use of the word "transport" here implies movement from one space to another, as do the words "traveler," "journey," "distance" and the apparent contextual definition of the word "world." A storyworld, in other words, involves characters, actions, events, but these can only occur within a "world,"—a place or space.

Herman's definition of storyworld relies on the same distinctions: it includes people and events, but takes place "in the world to which recipients [readers] relocate." In later chapters, Herman delves into what he regards as the central elements of a story: temporalities, spatialization, and perspectives—terms that might be translated to mean the time and events of a narrative, its space or setting, and the characters that participate in the events. However, he notes at the beginning to his chapter on "spatialization,"

> spatial reference plays a crucial, not an optional or derivative, role in stories. [. . .] Narratives should be viewed not just as temporally structured communicative acts but also as systems of verbal or visual prompts anchored in mental models having a particular spatial structure. More exactly, narratives represent the world being told about as having a specific spatial structure. (2004, 264)

Herman's explanation here not only privileges the space of a storyworld, but suggests that other elements—time, for example—are in actuality a product of the space in which they occur. So, for instance, an event can be regarded as movement across a given space.

In *Topographies* J. Hillis Miller glosses Martin Heidegger's work by focusing on the importance of place, especially in literature. As he writes there, "A novel is a figurative mapping. The story traces out diachronically the movement of the characters from house to house and from time to time, as the crisscross of their relationships gradually creates an imaginary space" (1995, 19). Miller applies this conception of fictional space to works by Hardy, Dickens, and Faulkner, but it might just as usefully be applied to a television series like *The Sopranos*.

I can now return to the beginning of this chapter, and to my initial question of just what it means for television producers and television audiences to think of a series as a "world." This kind of thinking draws on our innate understanding of art and especially narrative art as providing an artificial space, a "virtual reality." The desire to create and inhabit such spaces can be traced back as far as humankind itself, and further has been demonstrated to be part of our physiological makeup, a product of the way our brains operate. And while such spaces often include characters and objects, and involve actions and events, the base for that storyworld is the space itself. In this sense we might call the "world" of *Bates Motel*, or *M*A*S*H*, or *Game of Thrones*, a storyworld or a "virtual reality," but it comes in the end to the same thing: a space to which we as viewers relocate, a space we inhabit and explore.

NOTE

1. There is an argument to be made that not all forms of art are mimetic. Some craft art, for example, might be better thought of in practical useful terms, while works by Picasso and Duchamp might be labeled "symbolic" or "non-realistic." On the other hand, work by Pollack, apparently non-realistic, does capture the experience of his physical movements in making the marks on the canvas: it becomes kinetic. In any

event, this larger debate is beyond the scope of this book. Drawing on many of the writers and thinkers I have listed above, I take for granted here that art serves—at least primarily—a mimetic function.

Chapter 2

"Land Spreadin' Out So Far and Wide"

The TV Medium

In chapter 1, I use the terms "storyworld" and "virtual reality" to locate television within the broader context of art history and particularly the history of narrative. Like *Hamlet*, or *Great Expectations*, or even *World of Warcraft*, a television series offers us an alternative reality in which to exist. In chapter 2 I separate television out from this larger background, delineating its unique characteristics as a narrative medium, and exploring how these characteristics contribute to its ability to create space.

TV'S STORYWORLD PREDECESSORS

As a medium, television has many of the same elements we associate with other narrative forms. Like the novel or short story, for instance, a TV series involves characters, plots, settings, as well as irony, perspective, point-of-view, symbols and motifs, themes. So close are the two forms, in fact, that one can be transformed into the other with relative ease. A number of recent television series have been based on books or book series, including *Game of Thrones*, *Wayward Pines*, *The Last Ship*, *American Gods*, and *Quarry*. And while books based on television series are less common, *Star Trek*, *The X-Files*, even *Dallas*, have all lent themselves to novelization.

We might also think of narrative television as a species of drama. That is, in addition to text-based elements it utilizes visual and auditory channels of meaning. When we watch a drama we are not only aware of character traits and how dramatic irony builds suspense; we also notice how lines are delivered, where characters stand in relation to one another, and how lighting is used to generate emotion.

Yet television doesn't exactly work like either text-based fiction or stage plays.

Its nearest relative might be the cinema. On the most basic level, both involve moving images captured on film or video in one place, which are then broadcast through a screen to a viewer at another. An alien arriving on Earth likely wouldn't recognize the difference, at least on initial viewing.

And television might usefully be thought of as "cinematic" in the sense that, even beyond the auditory and visual elements it shares with the stage play, it also takes advantage of layers of meaning created by the recording process itself. Once a film or video camera is involved, a film-maker can alter our visual perspective on an image or scene. She might place the camera above or below the action; she might follow characters from behind or take us in a 360 degree circle around them; she might have us look at a face in close-up, or let us watch a train as it slowly travels miles over the length of a landscape. The recording process also allows her to juxtapose images in a way a stage play can't. She can show us a man walk into a burning building in one shot, in the next show him inside the building moving through the flames, and finally cut to a close-up of a baby lying in a crib on the building's second floor, blissfully unaware of the danger below.

Many of television's effects as a storyworld, then, might be traced to its cinematic aspect. These effects have, as John Corner points out, been exhaustively detailed by film scholars, resulting in "a rich and complex literature of commentary on ontological and evidential matters" (1999, 25). Sigfried Kracauer's *Theory of Film*, for example, is particularly instructive for thinking about moving images as storyworlds. His description of the film viewing experience prefigures later psychological approaches to narrative reception like Richard Gerrig's. Kracauer writes, for instance, "Lowered consciousness invites dreaming. [. . .] the moviegoer finds himself in a state between waking and sleeping that favors hypnoagogic fantasies" (1968, 163). Elsewhere he quotes French psychologist, Henri Wallon, who explains, "in the cinema I dissolve into all things and beings. [. . .] I identify myself with its images, because I more or less forget myself in what is being displayed on the screen. I am no longer in my life, I am in the film produced in front of me" (159). Wallon finds himself not "seeing" the film, but "in" the film, inhabiting the space presented before him, in Gerrig's terms "transported" into it. Kracauer's groundbreaking work originally appeared in 1960; post narratology, cinema studies have actually taken up the specific term "storyworld" as a means of describing film's effects. In *Ecologies of the Moving Image*, for example, Adrian Ivakhiv argues, "Cinema [. . .] produces and discloses worlds. It is cosmomorphic: it provides morphogenesis, the coming into form, of worlds" (2013, preface). Where Kracauer's experiential descriptions hint at "worlds," Ivakhiv's comments make those worlds explicit.

Kracauer additionally offers an explanation for how and why film impacts us emotionally and psychologically. Key to this explanation is film's "endlessness," a quality inherent in its movement: "Originally, film was expected to bring the evolution of photography to an end—satisfying at last the age-old desire to picture things moving" (1968, 27). A picture ends at the frame; a moving picture goes on and on. For Kracauer this movement makes film the experiential equal to reality—a second reality (indeed, Kracauer subtitles his influential work "the redemption of reality," suggesting film somehow *improves* on reality). In the same vein, Ivakhiv argues that "the art of the moving image [. . .] comes closest to depicting reality itself, because reality is always in motion, always in a process of becoming" (2013, preface). In visual terms at least, moving images replicate absolutely whatever happens to be in front of the camera. The claim these two writers make is for film as the most advanced artistic medium, precisely because it replicates reality so exactly. The same basic argument might be applied to television as well: moving images affect us in many of the same ways whatever the size of the screen on which they may be projected.

TV'S CHARACTERISTICS

Television is not synonymous with film though, and as Jason Mittell notes, television deserves to be addressed "on its own terms rather than in the language of literature or film" (2015, 16). For all its similarities to film, television is a fundamentally different medium. The heart of this difference is its sense of immediacy. I noted above that both forms "involve moving images captured on film or video in one place and broadcast through a screen to a viewer in another." Film, however, is virtually always recorded at an earlier point for later broadcast. As Corner points out, "unlike photography or cinema, there is [. . .] the possibility of 'instant' transmission in television, providing the medium with that 'liveness' which has been seen to be its defining characteristic" (1999, 25).

This "defining characteristic" is partly a remnant of television's history. In *Teleliteracy*, David Bianculli reminds us that television traces its genealogy just as much through radio as it does through film. And radio, as he points out, was and is principally about immediacy: "Almost from the start, radio operators recognized and exploited the value the medium's immediacy could give to news and sports: no more waiting for the next day's paper, or the latest newsreel, to see or hear what was happening" (1992, 47). The fact that many of the earliest television broadcast networks began as radio stations—NBC and CBS for instance—means live-ness was hardwired into television's DNA.

Though somewhat dated now, John Ellis's *Visible Fictions: Cinema, Television, Video* was among the first scholarly works to lay out in a systematic way the underlying differences between film and TV, and most of his arguments remain relevant. Ellis too begins from the premise that the most noteworthy difference between the two is television's ability to transmit live images. Like Kracauer, he ties film to photography, but he regards this connection as limiting rather than freeing: "Cinema," he notes "as a photographic medium instantly poses its images and sounds as recorded phenomenon, whose construction occurred in another time and another place"; in contrast, TV "assiduously maintains a general sense of the live and instantaneous nature of its presentations" (1992, 39).

Even a cursory glance at the two media makes clear this difference. "Cinema has never really been able to produce news" (Ellis 1992, 15), for example: the newsreel focused on events that were hopelessly dated in comparison to stories on nightly news programs, one reason why the newsreel disappeared as television gained in popularity. As for films themselves, they tended to focus on events or stories from history—the Western; the gangster film; *All Quiet on the Western Front*; *Gone With the Wind*. This distinction remains with film even today: *United 93*, a "topical" film appeared five years after 9/11. Captain "Sully" Sullenberger's miracle landing on the Potomac River took place in 2009; *Sully* appeared in theaters in 2016. Likewise, the Deepwater Horizon disaster, which occurred in 2010, wasn't portrayed on the silver screen until 2016. Film documents history; television documents the now.

Ellis and Corner are both quick to remind us that much of TV is recorded as well, particularly the kinds of shows I highlight in this volume: fictional narratives. However, the possibility that a show might be live, and the juxtaposition of scripted, recorded television with live non-fiction programming, lends to the scripted show an air of immediacy that can result in a particularly potent kind of storyworld. This was true of radio as well. Orson Wells's "War of the Worlds" broadcast took advantage of radio's connection to real-time events to produce a fictional program. Listeners invested so thoroughly in what they were hearing, believing it was "real," precisely because they confused the fact that it was happening "live" with its claims to reality.

And the potential for live-ness gives to even recorded programming a sense of immediacy. *Breaking Bad* may be entirely fictional, but in the context of a medium that can also let us watch live as the twin towers in New York fell, the show already feels more immediate, more live, than any film. In part, this sense of immediacy derives from the larger context of television programming. In part, this effect can be traced to what media scholar Raymond Williams termed "flow": the total effect of television programming, the impact of multiple images juxtaposed against one another, which tends to overwhelm the effect of any single show or series (2003). The larger context in which *Breaking Bad* appears—hundreds of networks broadcasting non-stop programming of myriad types, means the scripted show is surrounded on every side by news segments, sports broadcasts, commercials, as well as other scripted narrative. As Heath and Skirrow note, "The immediate time of the image is pulled into a confusion with the time of the events shown, tending to diminish the impression of the mode of presence in absence characteristic of film, suggesting a permanently alive view on the world, the generalized fantasy of the television institution of the image that it is direct, and direct for me" (1977: 53–4). "Flow" is a somewhat dated concept now, given our access to streaming services and DVR. Yet even given these new technologies, it remains true that television, unlike film, is surrounded on all sides by content. Even if we never watch commercials, for instance, we often watch a given program in the context of other programs—other series, the news. And Netflix, after all, presents our viewing possibilities together visually, in one complete list of images.

As Heath and Skirrow suggest, our sense of immediacy when watching TV is heightened by a second characteristic—its "domestic" quality. Ellis writes,

> The TV set is another domestic object, often the place where family photos are put: the direction of the glance toward the personalities on the TV screen being supplemented by the presence of 'loved ones' immediately above. Broadcast TV is also intimate and every day, a part of home life rather than any kind of special event. (1992, 113)

Cinema is a special event: we make plans to go before we actually go; once there we pay money to buy a ticket that gains us admittance; we sit in darkness, separated by that darkness from everyone and everything else around us. Television, on the other hand, is integrated into our daily routines. Not only does it usually reside in the central room of the house, but it may be left on twenty-four hours a day, a background soundtrack with images while we do our chores, eat supper, spend time with our families. The television Ellis writes about was a bulky console, situated in one room of the house, the opposite of portable. The fact that we can now access television programming virtually anywhere and at any time certainly changes how we access it—we are less often together with our family when we watch, for instance. Watching via our laptops or cellphones, though, only means television is even more integrated into our lives. We carry it with us; in some senses, we are now literally never without it; if anything it might be more accurate to call television "pervasive," rather than "domestic," but Ellis's point, that it is integrated into our lives, remains true.

"The medium is the message," of course, and Ellis makes this clear in his analysis—the differences between film and TV, especially their difference in immediacy, shape their content:

> film is known to be photographed, elsewhere and at an earlier time to the projected performance of the film. The institution of cinema assumes this in all of its workings: the practice of marketing by narrative image, the fact that films are still "new" for several months after their initial release, the reluctance to place precise dates on filmic events that are vaguely contemporary. Cinema is profoundly marked by what Roland Barthes has called the "photo effect," the specific and poignant way in which photographs create their sense of reality. In some sense, what has already been said about voyeurism, fetishism, and identification in relation to the gaze has specified some features of the photo effect, especially the irreducible distance between viewer and object. (58)

As a result,

> The predominant myth of cinema, fostered by cinema itself, is that its images and sounds present reality. The equivalent myth of TV is that its broadcasts are immediate and live. Each myth reveals something of how the medium concerned wants to be watched. It reveals the kind of spectator that the medium proposes that we should be, what state of mind we should have, what kinds of pleasure and satisfaction we should achieve. (77)

But if television events are not "special" in the way of cinematic events, Corner reminds us,

> This is not all a matter of loss. Television's scale, when combined with its typically domestic mode of reception and then its forms of spoken address, provides it with the grounds of a relaxed sociality simply unavailable to cinema. Part of this sociality is the sense of the television device as putting home and studio or home and world into temporary copresence. (1999, 26)

TV relies on a certain persistence, a persistence that encourages a form of addiction and that can affect us in ways just as powerful as the cinema. It is always there, its images repeated over and over. Lyndon Johnson fretted over Vietnam coverage, the fact that "many times each week [. . .] television brings the war into American homes" (qtd. in Hallin 1989, 103), and Nixon suggested America might never be able to fight another war in an age of television: "Whatever the intention behind such relentless and literal reporting of the war, the result was a serious demoralization of the home front, raising the question whether America would ever again be able to fight an enemy abroad with unity and strength of purpose at home" (qtd in Hallin, 1989, 3). The landscape of the war was not simply "over there," but in American homes, and it was there day after day, week after week. The effect worked not just with documentary subjects like war, but with fictional narrative on TV as well. Other cultural events spawned by television—J.R. Ewing's shooting on *Dallas*, the mystery over Laura Palmer's death on *Twin Peaks*, the series finales of *M*A*S*H*, *Newhart*, *The Sopranos*—these events had power not because they were spectacular in and of themselves, but because they sprang out of a slow build-up in audience fascination.

This power springs from TV's immediacy, from its domesticity, but also from the particular form its narratives tend to take: the serial. Of course, seriality was another consequence of television's roots in radio. Radio's rich tradition of serials included *Dick Tracy*, *Little Orphan Annie*, and *Superman*. In fact, some radio programs—*The Guiding Light*, *The Lone Ranger*, *The Jack Benny Program*—even survived the shift from one medium into another.

Seriality, like immediacy and domesticity but also in concert with them, lends the virtual space of the television program realism. Serials maintain a certain verisimilitude to life not available in a novel, a play, or a film, a verisimilitude attached to time. Series occur with frequency; they occur with regularity; and they are typically designed to be open-ended. In many ways soap operas, in fact, represent television in its purest form. They are not merely serial; they appear five days a week, every week, throughout the year. While this isn't quite the same as having a show that happens in real time *as* you live, it is the closest a medium has yet come to achieving this sense of reality. The sheer amount of time a fan spends in such a storyworld argues for its "reality." In some cases actors have essentially lived their entire lives on a show, blurring the lines between the real and the imagined even further and making these characters perhaps better known to viewers than members of the viewers' own families. Abigail De Kosnik calls these "lifelong stories," a phrase that highlights their status as alternative realities (2013, 355). William Roache, for instance, has played Ken Barlow on the BBC's *Coronation Street* for fifty-six years, while in America, Don Hastings played Bob Hughes on *As the World Turns* for just under fifty. Kimberly McCullough began playing Robin Scorpio on *General Hospital* at the age of seven in 1985, a role she has returned to off-and-on ever since. Fans of the series have watched her grow and develop as an actress, but surely her time on the series has also reflected important growth and development in her "real" life as well. And while most prime-time series can't lay claim to the kind of longevity soaps achieve, both *Gunsmoke* and *Law and Order* each lasted twenty years. For an audience, that means twenty years of participating in a single storyworld, week after week (in fact, if we include *Law and Order: SVU* as a part of the *Law and Order* universe, the series will soon begin its twenty-ninth season on the air).

As Ellis describes it, "Fundamentally, the series implies the form of the dilemma rather than that of resolution and closure. This perhaps is the central contribution that broadcast TV has made to the long history of narrative forms and narrativized perception of the world" (1992, 154). As Ellis suggests, the history of Western narrative is almost exclusively the history of a very particular kind of plot, one that begins with a problem that needs to be worked out, reaches a climax in the action and interest of the story, and eventually comes to a resolution. Television, in contrast, relies on the continuation of story, an open-endedness that fundamentally changes what gets told. The form is not absolutely open-ended: most shows do eventually end (though *General Hospital* shows no signs of stopping even after fifty-five years), and many shows rely on a single-episode or single-season structure that works much like a short story or novel with an introduction, building action, climax, and conclusion. Nevertheless these small-scale "endings" are undone by the fact that, on the larger scale, characters on TV continue on, whatever resolution in action a given story might reach at episode's end. This is at least one reason why fans so often feel let down by series finales (see audience complaints about the endings of *Seinfeld*, *The Sopranos*, *Battlestar Galactica*, never mind the countless shows that have been cancelled with no resolution whatsoever): television stories are made to go on and on. Ending them means disrupting their natural order—a conclusion necessarily feels too fast in the context of a long-running storyline, but more than this an ending violates the expectations for continuation we have developed over the course, sometimes of years, of watching.

Comments such as Ellis's make it tempting to see television as a kind of apotheosis of artistic technologies: the most exact replication of reality we have yet achieved. Adopting such a viewpoint, we might see art as one long evolution toward a human longing for absolute verisimilitude, or perhaps the kind of "ideal" virtual reality Marie-Laure Ryan uses as her touchstone. As Ryan suggests, both those who celebrate VR and those who fear it (echoes again of Aristotle and Plato) often make claims about its ability to replace reality. She quotes Michael Benedikt, an early organizer of VR conferences:

> Cyberspace's inherent immateriality and malleability of content provides the most tempting stage for the acting out of mythical realities, realities once "confined" to drug-enhanced ritual, to theater, painting, books, and such media that are always, in themselves, somewhat less than what they reach, mere gateways. Cyberspace can be seen as an extension, some might say an inevitable extension, of our age-old capacity and need to dwell in fiction. (2015, 36)

And Ryan herself sometimes makes such grand pronouncements as well. She writes, for instance about advances in the visual arts:

> All this changed when the discovery of the laws of perspective allowed the projection of three-dimensional space onto a two-dimensional surface. This projection opens up a depth that assigns spatial coordinates—the center of projection, or physical point of view—to the body of the spectator. Perspective painting immerses a virtual body in an environment that stretches in imagination far beyond the confines of the canvas. From the spatial point of view, the embodied gaze of the spectator experiences the depicted objects as virtually present, though the flat surface of the painting erects an invisible wall that prevents physical interaction. (2)

And of film she writes,

> In contemporary culture, moving pictures are the most immersive of all media. Until VR is perfected and becomes widely available, no other form of expression will approximate their ability to combine the spatial extension and fullness of detail of still pictures with the temporality, narrative power, referential mobility (jumping across space and time), and general fluidity of language. (85)

Adrian Ivakhiv argues that film has an "affective immersion that makes it more powerful than most other art forms" (2013, chapter 2). And Jason Mittell notes, "Few storytelling forms can match serial television for narrative breadth and vastness" (2015, 292).

Post-postmodern theory, though, we are taught to reject such broad-reaching narratives, the idea that perspective might make art "better," or that virtual reality might be the pinnacle of artistic technology. The notion that cave paintings represent a primal version of film or TV or VR certainly seems to argue against them. So too does the fact that older artistic media have not simply sat idle in the face of newer media. The novel continues to grow and develop, as evidenced in work from *Infinite Jest*, to *House of Leaves*, to *Lincoln in the Bardo*. Film's more recent innovations include THX surround sound, IMAX screens, and 3D.

Looked at in this way, we are encouraged to look at television's specific qualities as a medium, what it does in particular, rather than how it improves on other media. A novel has its own particular charms as a virtual storyworld; a film has different, but no less potent, charms of its own. Ryan, for instance, notes that "immersion in a book" is like "cinema in your head": "As the reader simulates the story, her mind allegedly becomes the theater of a steady flow of pictures" (2015, 85). This sort of immersion, in which the reader is allowed to co-create the world with the author, comes with a powerful sense of realism, one unavailable with moving pictures.

Film has its own power to "transport." In *Phantom Empire*, Geoffrey O'Brien writes movingly of the filmgoer's experience: "The movie screen, in its imperial habitat on Market Street, was considerably more than a window.

You had to pass through a number of intermediary zones—ticket booth, popcorn stand, usher's station—even to approach it. After passing through a region of silence and blindness the spectator slid into the seat and submitted to an unearthly visitation" (1995, 36). The theater isolates us from one another, forces the rest of the world to recede, making it easier for us to enter the cinema "simulacrum."

Yet even though it works in the complete opposite way, television offers an immersive experience of its own. If we recognize cinema's power springs from the isolation the viewer feels in his or her seat—the singularity of the experience—we must also recognize that TV's easy accessibility offers an immediacy that cinema can't match. Where cinema engulfs us in its "special" events, television insinuates itself into the viewer's life, a wholly different sort of realism. In short, and this might be said of all artistic media, often what helps move a reader into one medium's storyworld may be the antithesis of what moves a reader into another. Every medium operates most effectively by discovering its own specific nature.

Finally, though, if each artistic medium offers its own unique virtual experience, it is also true that they borrow from one another. That is to say, television's "unique" elements are not entirely unique. For all its centrality to television, for example, seriality is certainly not isolated to television. It shows up as an artistic technique in earlier art forms—the Victorian novel, for instance. It occasionally shows up in the cinema, from early series such as *The New Adventures of Tarzan* or *Flash Gordon Conquers the Universe*, to contemporary franchises like *Star Wars* or *Harry Potter*. Likewise, seriality is a quality of cartoon strips and comics.

The differences lie in the particular combination of effects specific to each medium. As Ellis writes, for example,

> There is a passing similarity between TV serials and series and the massive, often serialized novels that are the high point of the nineteenth century. Each is prone to the development of incident and detail rather than the concise narrative development exemplified by cinema films. Yet their overall architecture is different, with the novel's majestic synthesis of its characters and incidents (a characteristic of Dickens) contrasting with the fragmentary and often open-ended structure of the TV series. (1992, 64)

TV SPACES

Television's characteristics make it especially suited for creating spaces, spaces the viewer is invited to enter and explore. While it doesn't have the user agency that typically accompanies virtual reality, this aspect of TV does make it similar to the computer-based VR experience.

First, because it is serialized, an open-ended narrative, characters and plots are relatively de-emphasized in favor of setting. A given event in a series—Dexter's attempts to keep his serial killer life separate from his family life—may come to an end: Dexter's wife Rita is murdered by another serial killer, resolving this particular tension. After the event, though, the world of the series continues on. Characters in a series may rise and fall in importance, or may even leave a series altogether. Henry Blake, Trapper John, Frank Burns, and Radar O'Reilly all left at various points during *M*A*S*H*'s eleven year run; Diane left *Cheers*; Stringer Bell was killed at the end of *The Wire*'s third season; Glenn dies during the eighth season premiere of *The Walking Dead*—all of these series continued to grow and develop. Partly as a result, a series is actually under a certain amount of pressure to expand its space over time. But additionally, the open-ended nature of television narrative means remaining spatially static risks a world that feels claustrophobic. Character and events contribute to growth, of course, but audiences need to explore the world a series sets up if that world is to feel realistically complete. A film, in contrast, is more like a photograph in this sense: its plot structure pushes us to accept it as a "slice of life," while television's open-endedness cannot settle for this limitation.

Television's immediacy and domesticity contribute to the emphasis on space as well. First, TV's immediacy has to do with its ability to bring events happening at a distance to us, wherever we might be. As McLuhan noted, media is about extending "our senses and nerves" (1964, 80), and in the case of television, that means extending our ability to see and hear things at a distance. We can watch Tiger Woods play a round of golf at the Master's, hear him strike the ball, even if we aren't physically in Augusta, Georgia. In short, television as a medium, was designed to bring other parts of the world to us. But we don't have to do anything special to make this happen. That is, we can access those other worlds any time we want, from the comfort of our couches or from a seat in an airplane several thousand feet above the ground. Our world and the "other" world are fused in this sense through the screen; our space becomes the "other" space.

Finally, I conclude this chapter by making a direct comparison between film and television, one that I think demonstrates the importance of space to the latter. Alfred Hitchcock's *Psycho* (1960) is primarily driven by character. This is not to say that the spaces of the film don't matter. Among other things, Marion Crane's movement during the early part of the film from the city of Phoenix to the small town of Fairvale influences how we regard her situation. At first the shift seems to highlight the town's relative placidity, making of the country an idyllic escape from the city. Of course Hitchcock uses our expectations in this regard to his advantage, surprising us with the underlying viciousness that exists beneath the country's exterior.

But Hitchcock's reversal of our expectations is even more dramatic when it comes to the characters. He focuses tightly on a single character for the first third of the film, following Marion everywhere she goes. He goes so far as to put us into her mind, making us privy to her thoughts and emotions. We are all the more shocked, then, when she is killed suddenly less than half way through the film. As a film, *Psycho* pushes us to focus on character and when one is suddenly taken away the effect is dramatic. But Hitchcock doesn't do away with Marion in order to privilege some other aspect of the film—setting for example. Rather he replaces one character focus with another. In fact, this second character becomes an even stronger driving force for the remainder of the film as we first come to know Norman Bates and then, along with the group of characters at the end, try to work out what motivates such a personality.

If we compare *Psycho* to the series *Bates Motel* (2013–2017), a TV series designed as a prequel to the film, we quickly recognize that the emphasis on character has been shifted to one on the space in which the events take place. Even the two titles make this clear: "psycho" emphasizes a single person; "Bates Motel" emphasizes a particular place. Again, this is not to suggest characters don't matter to this show. Part of the show's thrill is our chance to see just exactly what events in Norman's young adulthood led him to become the monster he is in *Psycho*. And other characters matter as well, especially his mother Norma, with whom he has an unusual, unhealthy, bond. But in fact many of the characters matter here—Norman's brother, Dylan; Norma's brother, Caleb; Emily Decody; Sherriff Romero.

Bates, in contrast to *Psycho*, must turn the space itself into an important element, if only because it must fill a relatively larger amount of time—fifty hours as opposed to two. And over the course of the series, this is exactly what the producers do. The series begins with Norma and Norman's arrival in town, a move that turns the rest of the series into their—and consequently our—exploration of this world. Additionally, one of the key plot points throughout the series has to do with the space itself: having bought the Bates Motel as a new start to their life, Norma discovers in the first episode that a new bypass is to be built that will direct traffic away from the sleepy highway where the motel sits, essentially ruining its chance of attracting customers. In other words, *where* things are in this space matters.

And *Bates Motel* is not the only series to rewrite a film in this way, highlighting a narrative's space. The film *Buffy the Vampire Slayer* (1992), revolves primarily around Buffy herself and what happens to her. But Sunnydale matters to the series (1996–2003) in a way Los Angeles simply doesn't to the film. *Westworld*, *Friday Night Lights*, *12 Monkeys*—in each film the action takes center stage, but in the TV series based on the films, we are allowed to explore the *world* in which the events occur.

Television bears some relationship to film; it bears some relationship to radio, novels, short stories, plays. But like every other medium, television has a unique set of characteristics that shape what kinds of stories it can tell and how it goes about telling them. Television's immediacy, domesticity, and seriality mean its worlds—the virtual spaces it offers—become its most valuable narrative tool.

Chapter 3

"I'm the Map, I'm the Map, I'm the Map"

TV's Storyworld Techniques

In their introduction to *Television Aesthetics and Style*, Jason Jacobs and Steven Peacock argue for a particular approach to television studies, one that takes in whole series rather than just isolated moments. Their choice of metaphor is especially instructive, as it involves "living into" the spaces we find on TV:

> the television "houses" we get to return to again and again want us as long-term tenants, as we become in the offices of Sterling Cooper Draper Pryce. We live into their familiarity and notice the adjustments in décor, light, the way a house absorbs, reflects, and shapes the lives of its inhabitants. Only television does this so regularly, with such insistent promotion of familiar spaces, people and objects. [. . .] It is only by inhabiting the space as a dwelling, a home, that we get to know it intimately and thereby earn the experience from where the first springs of criticism may arise. (2013, 12)

Up to this point, I have been explaining the "architecture" of television, looking at it in terms of its outer structure. I have established the usefulness of thinking about television series as virtual spaces, as "worlds." I have also outlined how TV's particular characteristics as a medium help to create this emphasis on space. In this chapter, I focus on the spaces themselves and some of the many ways television goes about "decorating" its storyworlds, the ways it makes them "liveable." TV's chief tools in this regard are visuals and movement, but it is the variety of uses to which these two tools are put that provides the best sense of how space works on television. Of course, as I said in the introduction to this book, and as others have said before me, television is far too broad a medium to talk about in terms of absolutes. I make no claim that my list of examples in this chapter is complete, or that the approaches I highlight show up in every series. My goal here is simply to offer grounding examples of how television over time has come to think about itself, how it has come to recognize its strengths, and how it has come to utilize those strengths to its best advantage.

A HISTORY OF TV SPACES

Television seems always to have understood—at least on some level—the centrality of space to its impact as a medium. The characteristics I draw attention to in chapter 2—immediacy, domesticity, and seriality—were apparent to TV producers from the medium's inception. And from that inception, they have been experimenting with a variety of techniques designed both to emphasize those characteristics and at the same time minimize TV's weaknesses.

Early shows—*The Honeymooners* (1955) for instance—were limited in terms of the physical spaces they could show on screen (in part because the show was filmed live, meaning characters needed to remain in a relatively isolated space). The boundaries of the sound stage meant most of the action had to take place in the Kramden's kitchen. Had this been a one-act play such a setting would have served nicely. But as an open-ended series, one that had to continue over many episodes, a single location was almost unworkably restrictive. To partially overcome this problem, the show carefully situates its action in a specific location, a location that is real and easily recognizable—New York City. The city is repeatedly referenced in the series' opening credits where a moon rises over a painting of the New York City skyline. This reference, however brief, allows us to envision the larger space in which the apartment exists; we populate that larger space using what we already know of the city, even if we never actually see it.

Additionally, though, the show borrows techniques from stage drama in an effort to expand its space. The window in the Kramden's kitchen, for example, becomes a means of interacting with the outside world, of making that world real. In a number of episodes Ralph uses it to yell "up" at Norton who lives in the apartment above; in another episode Alice hurls kitchen items out the window at Ralph on the sidewalk "below." Other locations in the Kramden's neighborhood get mentioned with regularity—the bowling alley, the Raccoon Lodge—as markers of the world that exists beyond the couple's walls. And Ralph is a bus driver after all, meaning he is constantly moving through the city's streets; even if we never actually see those movements, they too help expand the show's landscape.

Later series trade on the importance of space in a more thematic sense. Among these are two of Paul Henning's so-called "rural" comedies, *The Beverly Hillbillies* (1962–1971) and its spinoff, *Green Acres* (1965–1971).

In the first of these series, Jed Clampett and his Ozark mountain "hillbilly" family discover oil on their property, a discovery that results in their relocation to the wealthier, more "sophisticated" Beverly Hills, California: as the opening theme song goes, "the kinfolks said, 'Jed move away from there.' Said, 'California is the place you oughta be,' so they loaded up the truck and they moved to Beverly." The situation of the show, then, and the source for most of its humor, is the contrast between these "backwoods" personalities and the completely other space in which they find themselves. They try to make sense of this new space, for example, by using the vocabulary available to them, a vocabulary connected to the previous space: so the swimming pool becomes the "cement pond" and when first hearing the word "smog," Jethro determines, logically, "I reckon it's a small hog." All of this only works comically if we, as the audience, understand both spaces and the broad differences between them.

And if one show could turn shifting spaces into comic profit, so could another. *Green Acres* works in the same way as *The Beverly Hillbillies*, only in reverse. In the opening episode we're introduced to Oliver Wendell Douglas, a high-priced Manhattan attorney who longs for nothing more than to become a country farmer. Like the Clampetts, he and his wife Lisa—who belongs in the country even less than Oliver himself—relocate from one space to another. In this case their relatively "civilized" background creates havoc as they attempt to navigate the space of Hooterville with its country store, its one-car train, and its television-watching celebrity pig. Whether Henning intended it or not, this later series improves on our ability to think ourselves into its space. While we *watch* the Clampetts try to make sense of their new environment, in *Green Acres* our perspective is the Douglases', and we navigate through Hooterville along with them.

Other series have used the same basic structure, what might be called the "fish out of water" plotline. *Gilligan's Island* (1964–1967), for example, relocates its characters to a deserted island. Here every character comes from a different background—sailor, science professor, movie star—but all of them must cope with having found themselves in a new space, separated from what they know, and again, we explore that space as they do. One of the continual sources of humor here is the many ways the castaways try to reproduce the "outside" world within the primitive world of their island. Both *Mork and Mindy* (1978–1982) and *3rd Rock from the Sun* (1996–2001) employ this premise as well, both using aliens to explore the space of planet Earth.

Hogan's Heroes (1965–1971) offers yet another way of emphasizing space, by turning that space itself into a commodity. Ostensibly trapped within the confines of Stalag 13, Hogan and his merry band of mischief-makers actually have all but unlimited access to the outside world through a warren of secret tunnels. In virtually every episode they manage to "escape" into this outside world in order to fulfill some mission for the Allies. Space then becomes a source of the show's dramatic irony and suspense in addition to its comedy, as the prisoners work to safeguard their secret spaces from their German "captors" and to travel through the world outside the camp without being caught.

And not only early sitcoms developed innovative ways of using space. *Route 66*, for example, combined single episodic spaces with a larger series space. Jeffrey Sconce has described *The X-Files*' use of innovative narrative structure, its alternation between individual episode plotlines—"monster-of-the-week" stories—and an overarching series-long "mythology" (2004). However, *Route 66* (1960–1964) used a similar narrative approach in the early 1960s. The overarching plotline is less fully developed than that of *The X-Files* (1993–2002); *Route 66* works much more like an anthology series, each episode designed as its own short story. Yet those stories remain connected by the central characters—Tod Stiles and Buz Murdock—whose travels around the country in their convertible jalopy help hold the series together. In this sense, the show became about their movement into larger and larger spaces, each episode pushing the boundaries of the space we know so that eventually all of America seems to become that space, one small community at a time. And later shows have used a similar structural approach, including *The Fugitive* (1963–1967), *The Incredible Hulk* (1978–1982), and *Quantum Leap* (1989–1993), which all involve characters who, while they deal with their own individual problems, also manage in each episode to get involved in someone else's life.

I turn in the next section, though, to more contemporary television. For while many early series did recognize the importance of their story's space, it nevertheless took some time for television to develop fully its most powerful effects. Jason Mittell has written of a rise in TV's "complexity," particularly in the early 2000s, pointing specifically to shows like *Alias*, *24*, and *Lost* (2015). Allrath and Gymnich, in *Narrative Strategies in Television*, trace this shift in complexity to the 1990s, but their argument is consistent with Mittell's:

> The analysis of recent TV series is of particular narratological interest, since during the 1990s TV series increasingly began to employ experimental narrative techniques like multiperspectivity and unreliable narration as well as innovative functionalizations of voice-over narration and audiovisual presentation of consciousness. (2005, 4)

While Mittell, and Allrath and Gymnich, focus on narrative structure, the same kind of complexity in how television treats space can be seen evolving over the same period.

Mittell is careful to point out in more than one place that he does not use "complexity" as an evaluative term: it is not "a synonym for *quality television*" (2015, 46). A "complex" series is not necessarily superior to one with a simpler structure. My own choice to focus on more recent series—series that use space in especially innovative ways—is likewise not meant to undermine the value (entertainment value, aesthetic value, thematic value) of *The Dick Van Dyke Show*, or *The Andy Griffith Show*, or *The Love Boat.* Nor does complexity always result in a satisfying storyworld. The history of television includes a long list of shows that pushed their audience too far too fast—*Flashforward*, for example, or *Sense8*. For all its influence on later TV, even *Twin Peaks* lasted only a season and a half before viewers could simply no longer follow the sprawling narrative and complicated spaces it tried to develop.

Like Mittell I am reluctant to say television storyworlds today use space "better" than series in the past. Nevertheless, I think television has more recently begun to understand how to make the most of this component. Early series felt an urge to build their spaces, but later series have learned how to use space to increasingly greater effect. Among other important differences, for instance, recent series don't simply take place in a given landscape, or even use that landscape as an important plot element. Rather the best shows manage to turn the exploration of these spaces into the content of the show, fusing space organically with plot so that as the plot unfolds we come to know more of the space in which it does so.

STORYWORLD BUILDING BLOCKS: VISUALS AND MOVEMENT

One of the most obvious means of focusing our attention on space is simply to name a series for the space in which it takes place. Listing just a handful of titles from the last thirty years demonstrates the importance of place on TV: *St. Elsewhere*, *Hill Street Blues*, *Cheers*, *General Hospital*, *Twin Peaks*, *Wayward Pines*, *Riverdale*, *Fargo*, *Broadchurch*, *Ripper Street*, *South Park*, *Deadwood*, *Portlandia*, *Everwood*, *Jericho*, *Evening Shade*, *90210*, *Melrose Place*, *Hawaii Five-O*, *Chicago Hope*, *Haven*, *Boston Legal*, *Sex and the City*, *Ozark*, *30 Rock*, *Quantico*. All of these titles emphasize where the action occurs, orienting us to a particular virtual world—even if we never see an episode of the show. Other show titles remind us of the particular spatial situation such as *Lost*, or *Under the Dome*.

As an example of "moving pictures," though, it is the visuals that most obviously draw us into a series' space. On the simplest level, *The Honeymooners*' strategies from 1955 have remained useful for establishing a series' location. Most sitcoms even now are typically limited in what they can show beyond the confines of the soundstage (though most of them manage to improve on *The Honeymooners*' single room). Shots of an exterior help establish this larger space in the same way that the opening credits of that show featured the New York skyline. Not only the beginning of a show, but every new location throughout an episode, can easily be set up with an exterior shot. *Everybody Loves Raymond* is relatively basic in its number of locations: most scenes take place in either Ray's house or his parents' across the street. At points when we move from one to the other, though, producers typically insert an outside shot to orient us. *Seinfeld* uses even more anchor locations in the course of an episode—Jerry's apartment, Monk's café, George's office at Yankee Stadium—but the strategy is the same. Even drama series sometimes employ this technique: *L.A. Law* became infamous for its long panning shots of Los Angeles, shots that appeared not only when a character relocated to a new space but every time an episode came out of commercial break.

More recent series have begun experimenting with how space might be conveyed. For example, wider, landscape shots—offering the kinds of panoramas once only associated with film—have become more common on television in the last several years. These offer us broad perspectives on a series' space. *Fargo* (2014–) uses these to great effect, showing us not only huge expanses of snow-covered frozen tundra but wide shots of small-town main streets or rows of suburban houses huddled together. We feel the bleakness of this virtual world; we live in it over the course of a season. *Game of Thrones* (2011–2018), whose space encompasses entire kingdoms likes to use panoramic shots as well. These may re-situate us in a new kingdom or may make a thematic point: showing us for example the insignificance of travelers in relation to the wide open spaces through which they wander.

Often a series' landscape is figured from above, giving us a complete sense of the space as well as a certain feeling of control over it. Throughout *The Walking Dead* (2010–) characters seem to seek out vistas, an example of how a contemporary show can sometimes build itself around its need to explore spaces. In the first episode we find central character Rick sitting on a hilltop near Atlanta trying to contact Morgan—his first friend, post-apocalypse—by radio. He eventually gives up, having received no reply over several days, but the fact he needs a raised area to get the clearest signal affords us as viewers a complete view of both the city and the countryside that surrounds it. By episode 2, Rick has traveled into Atlanta. There he spends much of his time on building rooftops, which allows both him and us to map out the city streets below. Later, in season 2 ("Bloodletting"), Rick stands with Herschel atop another hill, looking out over Herschel's farm as Herschel's daughter Maggie rides up from the distance. "This place is beautiful," Rick says softly, "I can't believe how serene it is. Untouched."

The first episode of *Once Upon a Time* (2011–), a show that revolves around fairy tales and spaces both magical and mundane, opens with a shot from above of a man on horseback galloping along a narrow strip of land between two halves of a sea. We eventually learn this man is Prince Charming, but the space matters first, before we know him. The space he travels is a natural, beautiful land unspoiled by industry or commercialism, an open land, a land to be explored over the course of a series. The shot from above helps to highlight that openness.

It is movement, though, exploration of spaces, as much as visuals themselves that allow us to feel the spaces we're in. J. Hillis Miller writes that,

> A novel is a figurative mapping. The story traces out diachronically the movement of the characters from house to house and from time to time, as the crisscross of their relationships gradually creates an imaginary space. [. . .] The houses, roads, and walls stand not so much for the individual characters as for the dynamic field of relations among them. (1995, 19–20)

Marie-Laure Ryan makes a similar observation, writing of Balzac's ability to "tie description to the moving body," which allows him to capture "the feel of a place in both its atmosphere and its topography without losing the reader in a descriptive thicket" (2015, 86). Movement's capacity to allow us to experience a storyworld, to gain an understanding of that world and its characters but to do so through exploration, is an especially important component of recent television series. In the best cases, series use it to tie action to the world in which that action takes place. At one and the same time, movement allows a series room—in a quite literal sense—to expand spatially over a large number of episodes.

In fact, the motif of roads and paths is one of the most common on television. It reminds us of the importance of movement to a world's expansion and growth; roads operate on the level of the plot to make that expansion actually happen. In the very first scene of *The Walking Dead*, we find Rick standing on a deserted road facing a gas station, an empty gas can in his hand. As with the opening to *Once Upon a Time*, we don't yet know Rick—we don't even know his name. What we do know from this scene is just how important movement will be to this series. The cars beside the station are burned out shells; this man's quest is for gas: the ability to move matters. In other early episodes, Rick rides a horse down the middle of a deserted interstate, headed into Atlanta. The other side of the highway, the outbound lane, is nothing but abandoned cars as far as the eye can see. An open path means something significant here: on a basic level it tells us the city is dangerous, since all the traffic was heading out rather than in when the apocalypse came. The fact that Rick is heading in the direction of the danger tells us something about him as well.

Movement remains central to this series' storyline in recent episodes. During season 4, the fellowship of characters we began with become separated from each other. However, each discovers a railroad track with signs along it that promise safety and shelter at a mysterious place called "Terminus." Here again, movement matters, especially toward a destination. But movement becomes even more important once we reach "Terminus" and realize it is a trap set by post-apocalyptic cannibals. "Safety" and "security" in this particular world are illusions; survival means remaining on the move.

The AMC series *The Killing* (2011–2014) opens with the main character, detective Sarah Linden taking a morning run along a wooded path. In the first season of *Secrets and Lies* (2015–2016), the murder takes place along another wooded path. The second season of *Preacher* (2016–) opens with the characters racing along an empty stretch of highway looking for God. *Fargo*'s first season opens on a deserted highway as well, though this time at night and beneath a heavy snowfall: we look out the windshield with assassin Lorne Malvo as the yellow dividing line goes by hypnotically in front of us. In the opening to *The Handmaid's Tale* (2017–), June, Luke, and their daughter Hannah flee along backwoods roads toward Canada hoping to escape the repressive religious government, Gilead, which has taken over the eastern coast of America. Netflix's *Man in the High Castle* (2015–), posits a world in which Japan and Germany won World War II and divided up America. In

Figure 3.1. Rick rides an empty interstate into Atlanta.
***The Walking Dead,* 1.1**

the first episode, Joe Blake, a resistance fighter from New York, heads across country in a truck full of cargo. On the other side of the country, in San Francisco, Juliana Crane receives a bus ticket to Colorado. We watch them both as they travel the road until eventually they meet and form the seeds of a resistance movement.

Movement within a series can happen in at least two ways. First, characters may move back and forth among individual landmarks. Every time Emma Swann in *Once Upon a Time* travels from her home on the outskirts of town into the main street of Storybrooke, she takes us with her. As she passes by town landmarks—Gold's pawn shop, Granny's diner, the sheriff's department where her father, Prince Charming, works as sheriff—we move with her; we think about the interiors of each location even if we don't go in them. In the end we feel the whole town of Storybrooke during such walks; we become part of this world by inhabiting it. The same effect occurs on *Twin Peaks* as we move between the sheriff's office, the Double D Diner, and the Great Northern Hotel; or on *Gilmore Girls* (2000–2007) as we move through Stars Hollow, ducking into Luke's diner, strolling the town square or stopping in at Doose's Market. As characters move between them, we come to understand the larger space of the series as a set of interconnected smaller spaces. AI expert Michael Heim notes of digital virtual spaces, "Home is the node from which we link to other places and other things. [. . .] Home is the point of action and node of linkage that becomes a thread weaving the multitude of things into a world" (1994, 92). True enough perhaps if the narrative is bounded. But a TV show, one that takes place over some length of time, must feature multiple "homes," a series of landmarks that together create the virtual storyworld for the viewer.

In a "complex" series, though, movement within a space can also give way to the pressure to move outwards into new spaces. A television series, because it is open-ended, must constantly find new vistas to explore. Sometimes development takes the form of events or character development, but more often it takes the form of movement into new landscapes. As I have already suggested, *The Walking Dead* is built on this principle of constant movement as the survivors search for safe locations. *Battlestar Galactica* (2004–2009) does the same in space. *Once Upon a Time* has taken us to New York City to say nothing of entirely other realms including Alice's Wonderland and Purgatory. *Preacher*'s second season begins with the characters fleeing the town where the first season was set. By the end of its first season, *Westworld* (2016–) has begun literally tearing down its spaces in preparation for new ones to be built.

COMPLICATED MOVES

More important than the space and movement themselves are the various uses to which shows put them. In fact, a number of spatial motifs have developed over the last thirty years of television. One has to do with spatial oppositions. As I mentioned above, *The Killing* begins with the lead character running along a forest path, but the woods aren't just where Linden runs; they are also where a young girl's murdered body is found, setting off the mystery at the heart of the first two seasons. This woodland area is deliberately set against the city of Seattle, which looms in the background—the two share a complicated relationship—one involving more than just pastoral landscape juxtaposed with industrialized city.

The series *Justified* (2010–2015) focuses on U.S. Marshal Raylan Givens. Givens's home is Harlan County, Kentucky, but in the pilot episode we find him working in Miami, Florida. Much like the Beverly Hillbillies, he has held on to his native culture, though in his case the choice is far more knowing and deliberate. As he walks up to a drug dealer sitting by a pool, the camera focuses on his cowboy boots and his hat. He carries a gun in a holster at his hip and his fingers brush across the handle like an Old West marshal just itching to draw on his opponent. More interesting than this initial contrast in spaces though, is Raylan's return to Harlan. After shooting the drug dealer in the first episode, he finds himself under investigation, and is relocated by the marshal's service back to Kentucky. There, he finds himself confronting the people and places with whom he grew up, and from whom he had tried to escape. Initially, then, we find him in a space that contrasts the one he is from, but even when he returns "home," he views that space with the eyes of an outsider, having now seen more of the world.

Another sort of spatial contrast happens between individual viewpoints on spaces and broader, overhead perspectives. In *Story Logic*, David Herman describes this as a contrast between the "tour" and the "god's-eye" view (2004). The first, of course, allows us to feel we are within the landscape, exploring it with the characters, experiencing it. But the overhead shot matters as well, allowing us to re-orient ourselves to the total space of a location, to gain a sense of control over the world we inhabit. Effective texts in Herman's opinion alternate between the two; television can do this visually. To return once more to the opening scenes of *The Killing*, we get both the path Linden travels and a wide shot from above, once she arrives at the end, of the Pacific Ocean and the city of Seattle. In the opening of *Fargo* we are at some points behind the wheel with Malvo, focused on the road before us, and at other times above the car, watching it from a place of objectivity as it careens through the night. As I have suggested, the most satisfying instances of this shift happen organically: Rick watches walkers from a rooftop in Atlanta; in *The Wire* (2002–2008), detectives monitor the drug trade on the street from rooftops in Baltimore—in such instances we gain access to the perspective above because the characters themselves travel to these raised points. As a result, we remain within the individual viewpoint even as we gain access to the overall viewpoint. We attain the "god's-eye" *through* the tour.

One important version of the "god's eye" view is the map. We can create these ourselves, as we read. J. Hillis Miller writes, for instance:

> Among these diverse forms of spatial mapping, the use of topography in narrative takes its place. Every narrative, without exception, even the most apparently abstract and inward (the stories of Maurice Blanchot or of Franz Kafka, for example), traces out in its course an arrangement of places, dwellings, and rooms joined by paths or roads. These arrangements could be mapped. They tend in fact to be mapped, at least implicitly, in the mind of the reader as he or she reads the novel. (1995, 10)

Ted Friedman makes a similar point about digital simulations, calling them a "map-in-time" with a narrative dimension (1995, 86).

In fact, on television these maps are frequently made explicit. Maps of Sunnydale show up throughout *Buffy the Vampire Slayer*'s run. Often, they serve as important plot elements: in the season 7 episode, "Same Time, Same Place," for instance, Willow and Anya sit in Anya's apartment, a map between them. They sprinkle powder over it, a powder that reveals every place in town that harbors a demon. They have a tool to use; we gain access to a "god's-eye" perspective.

On *Battlestar Galactica*, we are constantly seeing maps in one form or another. One of the most common of these is the "dradus," or radar, which shows us the position of fighters and battleships. The ship itself is our primary location for most episodes, and so we're shown several maps with the ship's layout. Fleet admiral Adama keeps the remnants of the colonies going after the cylons have devastated their homeworlds by claiming to have a map leading to Earth. In season 3, we're shown maps of New Caprica, the planet the humans decide to colonize, a planet eventually occupied by the cylons. One of these maps—a detailed plan for a rebellion—becomes central to the plotline when Ellen Tigh decides to betray her fellow humans by turning it over to the cylons.

In fact, maps appear almost everywhere on television. In some instances, they are to be expected, as in crime dramas, where maps might help detectives track a murder spree or pinpoint a killer's location. In the first season of *True Detective* (2014–), Rusty Cohle quits the police force and becomes a bartender, but we later discover ("After You're Gone") he has continued to work obsessively on the serial killer case. When we see the storage unit he has been maintaining as an office, its walls are covered with images and clippings related to the case, including a number of maps. In the final season of *Broadchurch* (2013–2017), the detectives consult maps to trace a suspect's movements on the night of an assault. Sometimes the maps belong to the bad guys: during a season 3 episode of *Justified* ("Guy Walks Into a Bar") drug kingpin Robert Quarles looks over a map of Harlan County as he discusses the best locations for his "Oxy clinics."

Maps can be magical, revealing not only the lay of the land but hidden dimensions of the space. In the third season of *Once Upon a Time* ("Lost Girl"), Peter Pan gives Emma a map of Neverland, which will supposedly show her the location of her son, Henry, once she accepts her own magical powers. *Sleepy Hollow* (2013–2017) is full of maps, including several of the town itself featured in the opening credits. In an early episode from the first season Ichabod and his partner Abbie discover a 1773 survey map of the town hidden in a sextant in the cabin ("The Lesser Key of Solomon"). In another they find a map to purgatory hidden in George Washington's grave ("Pilot"). In the third season, they use the "Blavatsky map," which, like Willow and Anya's map on *Buffy*, can locate demons ("I, Witness"). In the first season of *Stranger Things* Jonathan and Nancy go monster hunting using a map of the town Jonathan has torn out of the phonebook ("The Monster"). More memorably, in a second season episode, "Will the Wise," Will maps the upside down world's tunnels using crayons and sheets of paper he pastes all over his home.

Maps can help characters understand the space they find themselves in. As might be expected, maps are key to the series *Lost* (2004–2010)—in "Lockdown," for example, Locke sees the blast door map, which reveals the Dharma initiative locations scattered across the island. The map offers both him and us a tantalizing clue to the true nature of the island. In the final season of *Orphan Black* (2013–2017), Cosima finds herself held captive by a geneticist on another island. When she discovers a map that shows where sentries are posted, she is one step closer to escape, but we gain a greater sense of the island's space from having seen it. In the first episode of *Altered Carbon* (2018–), main character Takeshi Kovacs awakens in a new body, in a world 200 years into his future. He needs to understand this new world, and so do we. The man who hires him, Lauren Bancroft, helps clarify it for both of us: gesturing to a world map, he explains he was "born in London," but later moved to "what was then called the United States." Maps even show up in children's television shows, as my headnote for this chapter suggests. Each episode of *Dora the Explorer* (2000–2015) involves Dora moving through a series of landmark locations toward a final goal; Dora always relies heavily on the character of the map to explain those landmarks and to get herself and her friends safely to the goal.

In the absence of maps, other series use titles to alert us to exactly where we are in space. Each scene of *Law and Order* and its various spinoffs begins with a title card listing the precise address where we are in this virtual version of New York City. So too, *The X-Files* offers a small title in the lower left hand of the screen, giving both the location and time of every new scene. *Fringe*, a series indebted to *The X-Files*, takes these place markers even further, integrating them into the particular space, fusing them with the landscape. TV series *24* (2001–2010) is a show about time, as the title itself makes clear, but it is equally about space. While it is true the clock appears on the screen at numerous moments throughout an episode, almost as common is the multiplied screen shot, where we're shown two, three, four spaces at once. In fact, most often these two tropes appear together, so that we see exactly what is happening at any given moment, but in multiple locations. The result: we can track the movements of characters in space, and think about them all at once as though they were figures on a map.[1]

As an aside, I might point out the many series maps that have been created outside of shows, maps that testify to our desire to understand the spaces we visit on television. Maps of the town Wayward Pines, for instance, show up throughout the series, but in addition to these, in conjunction with the series premiere, *Entertainment Weekly* published a map of the town. In 2014 Google Maps introduced a feature that allowed users to see both map and street views of Emmy nominated TV series filming locations. And fan-generated maps for all kinds of shows can be found all over the internet, from maps of the island on the *Lostpedia* wiki to interactive Google maps of *Game of Thrones*' Westeros, to a map tracking Bob Newhart's path to work during the opening credits of *The Bob Newhart Show*, and Inaki Aliste Lizarralde's detailed floor plans to TV apartments including Jerry Seinfeld's, Mary Richards's, and Bert and Ernie's.

The "tour," to use David Herman's term, is sometimes given another twist, when the beginning of a series finds a character discovering a location, as in the two Syfy series *Eureka* and *Haven*. In the first episode of the former, U.S. Marshal Jack Carter manages accidentally to stumble upon the hidden town of Eureka, a scientific community that works to create high tech gadgets for the government. He becomes embroiled in a series of time and space anomalies related to a tachyon accelerator, and by the end of the episode has been installed as the town sheriff. The result is we "discover" this town—the series' virtual space—along with him. Similarly FBI agent Audrey Parker discovers paranormal secrets when she is assigned to investigate a case in Haven, Maine. Emma Swann discovers the town of Storybrooke, Maine, arriving in her distinctive yellow VW Beetle, a car that will remain an important touchstone over the course of *Once Upon a Time*. Norman Bates and his mother arrive to the town of White Pine Bay in the pilot to *Bates Motel*. In *Walking*

Dead we begin with Rick Grimes waking up in a hospital to find the world has changed completely. And, as I mentioned above, *Justified* complicates this formula by having Raylon Givens arrive *back* in his home state after having been away for some time. In each case, we enter the new space along with the central character, discovering it as she does.

As I suggested, camera work may play an important role in introducing these spaces, but special shots can also sometimes influence how we feel about a given space. In the *Sopranos* (1999–2007) episode, "College," we begin at Bowdoin, where Tony waits for Meadow to finish her application interview. The opening shot of the episode moves us 360 degrees, completely around Tony, and in that 360 degrees we see the buildings of the campus, the quad, students walking back and forth—a setting clearly different from the ones we're used to. But this circular movement around Tony finishes with a straight on shot of the man himself as he puts a cigar into his mouth. There is something in his face when at last we reach it that indicates he isn't comfortable in this space. He feels out of place, bemused. When his daughter shows up his unease is further apparent in the dull joke he makes about the classes she's interested in, and his quick efforts to quell her excitement: "It's just an application." All of this sets up an episode where movement is essential to the plot, both in the sense that Tony and Meadow travel together from school to school, and in the sense that Tony must navigate carefully between the spaces of his job and the spaces of his family life.

The original British version of *Life on Mars* (2006–2007) uses a similar 360 degree shot early in the first episode, to set the scene and then to upend our expectations about that space. The episode's action begins in contemporary Manchester, where Sam is involved in a manhunt. We see row houses—indicative of a certain sort of neighborhood—and Sam chases a perp through a back alley, helping to emphasize the feel of this space through paths and his movement on foot. Before we even arrive at these row houses though, the first shots we get are taken from the wheel well of Sam's car as he speeds toward the crime scene. We see all of Manchester spread out behind him, but we see it from a very particular viewpoint—moving for sure, but with an emphasis on the car itself. In fact, later the car becomes important to the plot, moving Sam from one time to another, one world to another. Later in the episode, Sam stops his car at an underpass to collect his emotions, and as he steps out of it, another car runs him down. This event triggers the shift for Sam from the early 2000s to the 1970s. When he awakes and stands up, we're given another 360 degree shot, and much like the one in *The Sopranos*, this shot lets us know almost immediately that we're in unfamiliar surroundings. The houses behind Sam are half-demolished, representing a period when the city struggled with poverty and high crime. Sam's clothes have changed to those of another era as well. And behind him we find another car, though this one is very different from the contemporary sports car he was driving before.

Likewise, the British series *Broadchurch* begins with atypical shots. Most of the first images establish the location through a series of landmarks—the empty main street of town, the police station, the sea. But the sea is especially important to this series as it goes on, and in these opening moments the camera finally settles on Danny, a young teenager, who stands on the edge of a cliff overlooking the beach. We move toward him from behind, almost sneaking up on him, and then the camera rises up, over his head, so that we are looking straight down into an abyss; we have become him; we feel what he feels about this space. The moment, and the spot where it occurs are central to the mystery at the heart of the series, and we get that spot right from the beginning, but we're also told clearly how to think about it. This is a scary moment, not only for the long drop Danny faces but for the darkness that seems to swallow up his view so that he can only hear the crash of waves upon the shore below. The same moment, the same camera movement, gets repeated in the final season of the series, when we find Danny's father, still grief-stricken over his son's death, standing in the same spot and contemplating his own suicide.

A different effect is achieved when a show uses a "real" space as the inspiration for its virtual one: Harlan County, Kentucky, in *Justified*, Baltimore in *The Wire*. Such instances work in a postmodern way to confuse our sense of the real and the virtual. On the one hand, a show like *Fargo*, set in real locations in the upper Midwest, encourages us to think of the fictional story as

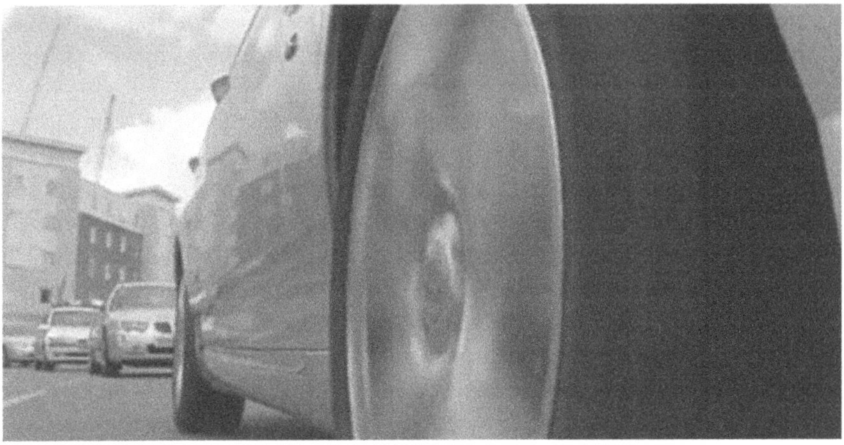

Figure 3.2. Contemporary Manchester, seen from Sam's wheel well. *Life on Mars (U.K.)*, 1.1

"real," (as does the text that appears at the beginning of each episode insisting "This is a true story"). On the other hand, a show like *Law and Order* is set in New York, yet many of the addresses given in the scene bumps lead to spots somewhere in the middle of the Hudson River. Fiction masquerades as the real, but the real also masquerades as fiction. The confusion of spaces, real and virtual, allow this to occur (for more on this effect, see chapter 8).

Another unusual use of space involves screens within the screen. In *Homeland* (2011–) the use of surveillance equipment in a given episode serves several functions at once. First, it allows us to look in on a location, and to think about one location while we are in another. It connects spaces, broadening out the total landscape. It also helps us to map out the spot being surveilled. In the case of *Homeland*'s first season, Carrie is keeping an eye on the Brody family's home, and has cameras set up throughout their house. We watch Carrie watching them on a screen split into four quadrants. Each quadrant shows us a different location in the house. As with *24*, we can see the whole house and what people are up to inside it, almost as though we were looking at a map. In fact, even when we see the family in "real" action, we filter what we see through those black-and-white images on Carrie's monitor; the awareness of the double space remains with us.

But the surveillance serves a broader purpose: it reminds us of what we ourselves are doing. Carrie watches the Brody family, tracking their movements through a particular space. In the same way, we track Carrie, Saul, and all the other characters' movements through the space of the series. In some ways, Carrie's surveillance helps teach us about the space we are watching and the relationship we should maintain to that space. If Carrie believes she is watching a criminal, to some extent we enter that same mindset—we follow Carrie and Saul, watching *them* when they believe *they* are hidden, seeing *them* skirt the law, make poor choices. We are the detective as much as Carrie is, and we are just as much the voyeur as well.

Finally, as Mittell notes, movement over the course of a series can happen in yet two more ways. For the most part I have been discussing what he terms "centrifugal complexity," in which the narrative, and consequently the space in which the narrative is set, pushes outward. As he rightly points out, however, a show can also utilize "centripetal complexity" (2013, 45–56). He uses the series *Breaking Bad* (2008–2013) as a prime example of a show that, rather than move outward offering us a broader and broader view of its spaces, moves inward, focusing specifically on a character's internal psychological development. Yet this doesn't mean *Breaking Bad* lacks a virtual space. Indeed, to a certain extent, Mittell's example helps to prove my larger point about television's storyworlds. For even a show that is so deeply focused on Walt's psychological development must still generate a space in which that development can take place. Albuquerque, of course, does matter to the series, as does the desert where Walt and Jesse park their RV, an empty space where the characters on at least one occasion find themselves trapped. But more important than this background is the way the producers will sometimes zoom in on miniature landscapes, turning them into highly charged spaces. At the beginning of season 2, Walt and Jesse find themselves trapped at drug-dealer Tucco's house in the desert ("Seven Thirty-Seven"). This gives the show another chance to highlight the wasteland backdrop, the impossibility of escape encoded in the vastness of that landscape. But after a quick shot of the desert, the camera picks out individual patches of ground, turning these into their own landscapes. Small objects become enormous: a baby's rattle, spent shell casings half buried in the sand, a piece of scrub brush. The effect is monstrous: a further emphasis on Walt and Jesse's inability to move—they are being held captive by Tucco and his aged father—but also on the madness that being trapped creates, where the miniscule becomes all of the world they can see.

In the end, the movement of characters in this series comes to resemble that of the fly featured in episode 10 from the third season. The fly is trapped, though it does not seem to realize it—it moves about within the confines of the meth lab where Walt works. That space is developed in tremendous detail, but ultimately the fly can't escape these four walls. This, of course, doesn't undercut the fact that an episode such as this one offers intense character development, but that character development is crucially connected to

Figure 3.3. A baby's rattle lies abandoned in the desert sand.
***Breaking Bad,* 2.1**

the way the space is developed. It is our virtual experience of that space as enclosed that allows us to feel that character development.

At this point I have not only established the importance of space for television but also delved into how shows go about utilizing this element, creating and building its spaces, making them real for us and creating opportunities for us to experience them in deep ways. Even so, I have not yet undertaken to examine "whole series" as Jacobs and Peacock advocate. Over the next several chapters, then, I focus in on specific genres and series, examining in greater detail how individual shows build their spaces over time.

NOTE

1. In fact, *24* offers an interesting contrast between film and television. Just a year before *24* premiered, the film *Timecode* experimented with a similar effect. The entire film is split into four quadrants, and we watch four different events taking place at four different locations simultaneously. Yet where *Timecode* offers an interesting conceptual experiment, ultimately it moves too slowly, unsure how to fill the various events in the quadrants, apparently unwilling to over-stimulate the audience. The TV series *24*, on the other hand, takes advantage of television's relatively longer format to develop its multiple locations so that when we see four at once we are less confused.

Chapter 4

"Same Bat Time, Same Bat Channel"

Opening Credits

Every storyworld must have some means of moving us into its space, a means of getting us from here to there, of "transporting" us, to use Richard Gerrig's word—into its alternate reality. Narrative theory uses the term "deixis" to talk about how this happens with a text. Because of its seriality, though, television doesn't just begin once; rather—as *Batman*'s famous episode-ending words remind us—it begins over and over again. Further, because a television episode is not generally an isolated event but rather surrounded by television's programming "flow," we tend to move fluidly in and out of a series' storyworld. Each episode, then—whether it occurs every day, as in the case of a soap opera, every week, as in the case of most primetime series television, or for just a few weeks out of the year as is increasingly the case with cable and streaming series—must move us back into its space, must re-situate us in that space and re-familiarize us with its landscape. One of the most powerful tools for achieving this transportation is the opening credit sequence. In this chapter, I examine how this particular device works to move us into a television storyworld.

GETTING THERE FROM HERE: DEICTIC SHIFT THEORY

The original usage of "deixis" relates to the pointing or specifying function some words possess. Mary Galbraith explains deixis has to do with subjectivity in language, how we use language to structure our personal experiences of the world: deictics "designate those words and aspects of language that can only be understood with reference to a NOW, a HERE, and an I [. . .]. Deixis is a language universal that orients the use of language with respect to a particular time, place, and person" (1994, 20–21). When we engage in a communication act, we must constantly provide orienting cues for those with whom we are communicating. Such terms are generally context-specific: they represent an agreement between the speaker and the listener about the nature of the situation in terms of when it occurs, where it occurs, and who is speaking. Or put another way, deictic words indicate a situational context upon which both participants are agreed, a shared *space* of communication between the speaker and listener.

As narrative theory became more interested in storyworlds as a subjective experience, both for the teller and the hearer, critics took up deixis as a useful way of thinking about how writers introduce readers into storyworlds and how readers utilize these cues to re-create those storyworlds in their own minds. Much of this critical history is summarized in *Deixis in Narrative* (1994), a comprehensive report on the work of the Discourse and Narrative Research Group working at the Center for Cognitive Science at SUNY Buffalo. In keeping with narratology studies, generally, this group included researchers from a broad variety of fields, including artificial intelligence, philosophy, linguistics, psychology, communicative disorders, education, English, and geography. Yet as editors Duchan, Bruder, and Hewitt point out in their introduction, all who participated in this long-term study were united by their belief in the "subjective nature of the storyworld experience" (1994, xi); in short, all saw narrative as producing virtual worlds.

What the collective eventually developed they called "Deictic Shift Theory." As Erwin Segal explains it, "We think that much of the detail of text is only understandable from a position somewhere within the narrative world requiring a deictic shift" (1994, 14); to understand the world a text creates we must be inside it. Further, "Deictic Shift Theory states that in fictional narrative, readers and authors shift their deictic center from the real-world situation to an image of themselves at a location within the story world" (15). In psychological terms, readers "transport" themselves into the narrative landscape. DST theorists "attempt to specify some mechanisms and computational processes that could implement" this transportation (15).

Deictic Shift Theory offers important clues to understanding narrative and storyworlds in general by identifying specific means through which we enter the fictional universe. It suggests that this process is the most essential to establishing a working, believable virtual reality. But how might we apply DST to television? *Deixis in Narrative* makes little mention of TV. Duchan, Bruder, Hewitt and their research collective do consider how deixis might be applied to artificial intelligence and AI-generated digital stories—virtual reality strictly defined—but they don't take up the question, in any meaningful way, of how it might be applied specifically to visuals and visually-based narratives.

To make that connection, I turn to another set of theorists, those interested in how we as humans experience visuals. Mark Johnson (*The Body in the Mind* 1990) and George Lakoff (*Women, Fire, and Dangerous Things* 2008) have posited what they refer to as "Kinesthetic Image Schemata" to help explain how we respond to visual worlds. Specifically, they argue that through reference to our own body we can achieve the kind of storyworld orientation in relation to visuals that language allows us to achieve with written texts.

Lakoff defines a number of these image schemata, beginning with the "Container Schema." As he explains it, we understand the concept of "in and out" because we regularly experience this concept kinesthetically: "we experience our bodies both as containers and as things in containers (e.g. rooms) constantly" (271). In terms of our visual perception and our ability to make sense of visuals as "worlds," Lakoff writes, "The visual field is understood as a container, e.g., things *come into* and *go out of sight*" (271). Likewise we understand frames and the way the edges of a painting or a photograph designate the "inside" and "outside" of the field we are meant to experience. We can imaginatively insert ourselves into visual fields, comprehend the objects we see and experience them subjectively, because when confronted with them we have a kinesthetic experience that allows us to think these visual relationships metaphorically through our own bodies: schemas are "inherently meaningful because they structure our direct experience" (272).

Other image schemata from Lakoff include "The Part-Whole Schema," "The Link Schema," "The Center-Periphery Schema," and the "Source-Goal-Path Schema." Each of these serves a different function in helping us "enter" our visual surroundings, whether those surroundings involve our day-to-day literal experience of life, our experience of a Degas painting, or our experience of an episode from *Once Upon a Time* (see also my discussion of "mirror neurons" in chapter 1).

Warren Buckland applies Johnson's and Lakoff's ideas to film analysis in his article, "Orientation in Film Space." Buckland, like other narrative theorists I have mentioned, sees a clear psychological relationship between readers and the fictional worlds they experience, a relationship he then looks for in cinema: "spectators are *necessarily* oriented in a film's fictional space by perceptual relations, they are imaginatively placed in direct relation to fictional objects" (2003, 90). He further suggests that Lakoff's schemata might usefully be applied to thinking about how viewers enter film storyworlds, using the idea that "*perception* is embodied by grounding it in the physical body" (91). Within the scope of this particular article, Buckland focuses generally on spatial "orientation," writing of this orientation in terms of deixis: "The spectator's deictic reference point in real space is shifted to an imaginative reference point when watching a film" (94). Deixis then doesn't merely apply to textual narratives, but to the moving image as well.

Erwin Segal's contribution to the *Deixis in Narrative* project, "A Cognitive-Phenomenological Theory of Fictional Narrative," focuses on what he terms "Edgework" in narrative, the elements that surround the narrative and help to initiate the deictic shift:

> In order to enter a storyworld, the reader must have, located in a mental space, a cognitive representation of the phenomenon that he or she is to experience. When the first sentence of the first chapter of a novel or short story is being read (or the curtain opens on a play, or the words "feature presentation" are replaced by a scene at the movies), a reader usually responds by anticipating that what comes next will represent a new entity. (1994, 75)

The "edgework"—the elements we recognize as physically framing the work—operate in Segal's conception to initiate deictic shifts. In his book *The Cognitive Semiotics of Film* (2007), Buckland makes a similar argument about the cinema, using Lackoff's "Container" schema specifically to argue that our innate experiential understanding of "in and out" allows us to utilize cinema cues—screen, frame, darkness of the theater contrasted against the light of the screen—to enter the world on the screen before us. Elsewhere, to illustrate his point, Buckland examines the opening of the Hitchcock film, *North by Northwest*, taking special note of how certain effects—the movement of the MGM logo for instance—"simulate an interaction with the fictional space," "the first stage in the transition from the non-fictional to the fictional level" (2003, 99).

I make a similar claim here: TV's opening credits serve as "edgework," shifting us deictically into the world of a series each time we begin a new episode. And to some extent I think Buckland's analysis offers a useful model for thinking about how this occurs. As he argues, the Container Schema helps explain how we are drawn "into" a series' space. However, as I've suggested before, television programs differ in many significant ways from films, and by the same token, television credits are often very different from the opening credits in cinema. For one thing, films typically open in a grander fashion than most TV shows, in keeping with the fact that they are made to be seen only once: a film is, so to speak, a self-contained object. The establishing shots that occur behind film credits are often long and steady—the three and a half minute single shot of a Mexican border town that begins *Touch of Evil*; the long overhead shot of Peter O'Toole mounting a motorcycle that introduces *Lawrence of Arabia*; the two minute tracking shot of a feather that opens *Forrest Gump*. The music that accompanies these shots often develops a heightened sense of emotion as well, from John Williams's pulsating *Jaws* soundtrack, to Dave Grusin's contemplative *On Golden Pond* theme, to Mancini's slinking *Pink Panther* score. A film must take us quickly, deeply into its world, and its credits must be designed to accomplish this task.

In contrast, television is episodic; that is, it works in terms of longevity, patiently spinning out over time. In addition, we view most shows in the context of Raymond Williams's "flow": in other words, we move fluidly in and out of a show. That show may be surrounded by other programs, or frequently interrupted by commercials or news briefs. Even in today's world of streaming services and DVRs, television is designed to stop and start; series aren't thought of as isolated entertainments but rather as strands in a complicated storyworld quilt made up of all the series we watch. Among the most obvious differences with film credits then—TV credits are made to be repeated. They are more familiar, and their job is less to introduce us for the first time to a large-scale storyworld than to re-introduce us to a show we're already comfortable with, that we already know. For this very reason, many shows' pilot episodes forego the credit sequence since in the beginning we don't yet know enough about the storyworld to be smoothly transported into it. Likewise, most streaming services have a function that prevents the credit sequence if we binge watch several episodes in a row; if we simply remain in the storyworld we don't need to be deictically shifted into it.

So while the Container Schema may work well for thinking about the cinema, a different image schema—the Source-Path-Goal Schema—seems more appropriate for talking about television deixis. Lakoff argues that in terms of our bodily experience, "Every time we go anywhere there is a place we start from, a place we wind up at, a sequence of contiguous locations connecting the starting and the ending points, and a direction" (1990, 274). Television is about continuity. As we've already seen, one of the chief characteristics of a series is its open-endedness. This has an effect on how stories are told, but additionally it shapes how we experience the space of that story. A television series moves in a direction, temporally and spatially, along what we might think of as a path. Lakoff thinks in terms of a beginning, middle, and end; television struggles with endpoints, but the basic notion of moving along a path serves as a useful analogy for thinking about TV series. In fact, as I have already pointed out, paths, landmarks, maps—these have important functions in the television narrative. So too it makes sense to think about opening credits as a kind of path we traverse into a show, one that re-familiarizes us with that show's landscape. We don't simply move "in" and "out" of them as we do with a film, but rather re-enter them.

TV CREDIT SEQUENCES: A BRIEF HISTORY

Interestingly, if we look at a selection of opening credit sequences over time we can actually chart television's evolution, particularly in terms of how it thinks about space.

Early series often focused, for example, on the actors during their title sequences, a holdover from vaudeville and radio, where the actors—Bob Hope, Judy Garland, W. C. Fields—were often the primary reason the audience turned up or tuned in. *The Honeymooners*, which first appeared as a stand-alone series in 1955, begins each episode with a roughly drawn picture of the New York skyline, but the camera quickly pans up to a shot of the moon, which is first filled with Jackie Gleason's rounded face and then his name. Gleason is established as the star even before the name of the series has been mentioned. The rest of the sequence includes only the additional names of Art Carney, Audrey Meadows, and Joyce Randolph. Of course, this opening reminds us that *The Honeymooners* actually began as a series of short sketches, first on CBS's *Cavalcade of Stars*, which Gleason hosted, and later on *The Jackie Gleason Show*. These programs were holdovers from the stage and particularly vaudeville, where stars were the prime attraction.

Similarly, the credits for *I Love Lucy* (1951–1957) feature only a heart placed over a stylized piece of fabric, the names of the two principles—Lucy and Desi—written across the heart before they dissolve into the series title. Other early series offer slightly more setting in their credits—the second season credits of *Leave It to Beaver* (1958–1959), for instance, feature Ward and June Cleaver at the base of the stairs handing out school lunches to Wally and the Beaver. Here again, however, the focus remains on the actors, with "Jerry Mathers as the Beaver" getting most of the emphasis. *Alfred Hitchcock Presents* (1955–1962) opens with the famous caricature of the director, into which he himself steps; *Perry Mason* (1957–1966) begins in its primary setting—the courtroom—but here again we see only minimal action in most versions of the credits, characters seated at tables looking anxious as Perry delivers a brief to the judge: the focus remains on the names of the actors themselves. *Gunsmoke*'s (1955–1975) credits are minimal as well, featuring James Arness riding a horse full tilt—though toward what we aren't told—while the announcer boldly intones, "Gunsmoke, starring James Arness as Matt Dillon."

As television evolved, later shows combined this emphasis on star power with an almost equal emphasis on characters. By now TV had become associated with the stereotyped character, a nod to the fact that, while series, these programs remained committed to self-contained episodes. *Gilligan's*

Island (1964–1967) actually emphasized the importance of stock characters in its theme song: "the millionaire and his wife; the movie star; the professor and Mary Anne . . ." Early seasons of *Happy Days* (1974–1984) featured characters' faces with the actors' names in the middle of a spinning .45 record. Later seasons had the characters "mugging" to emphasize their stock personalities and to play on audience expectations. This approach wasn't just limited to sitcoms: *The Love Boat* credits from 1982 feature a confident-looking Captain Stubing, a flirty Doctor Bricker, and an enthusiastic bartender, Isaac, who mimes a "gotcha" at the camera.

As I suggest in chapter 3, this doesn't necessarily mean shows from the 1950s, 1960s, and 1970s didn't understand the value of space on television. *Gilligan's Island*'s theme song, for instance, gives us the story each week of how these characters wound up on the island—the show's central setting—and ends with a shot from above of the castaways sitting at the lagoon. The beginning of every episode takes us to this location again. *All in the Family* features a montage of New York, as *The Bob Newhart Show* does with Chicago and *The Mary Tyler Moore Show* with Minneapolis. Yet as these latter show titles suggest, even when space is suggested in these examples, personalities remain central.

"COMPLEX" TV CREDITS

Only with the coming of the television arc, did series really begin to feature the show's space in the opening credits. The rise of the arc meant that long-term the characters and events of a series were headed somewhere, that they wouldn't just start over in the next episode. As a result, the series' space might be fully explored, and the credits seem to acknowledge this shift. Actors and characters suddenly matter less to the audience than the landscape they inhabit.

Twin Peaks was among the first non-soap series to develop a continuing storyline: the quest to solve Laura Palmer's murder. In keeping with that shift in structure, its opening credits were unique to the time as well. Each episode begins with a slow montage of the town. On the one hand, this montage tells us very little about the show's plot or characters. Indeed, it spins out as one of the slowest, least active opening title sequences in television history, a full minute and a half of shots of the mountains around the town, the sheriff's office, the Great Northern Hotel. And significantly, while many of these locations connect to people, no people ever appear. Even at the sawmill, where we watch a saw bite into a log, no one is there to operate that saw. On the other hand, the slow march of images gives us, one landmark at a time, a sense of the space we will visit for the duration of the episode. We begin with a marker of place, the town's welcome sign, welcoming us as viewers into this space, and we slowly push into the various nooks and crannies that make up the virtual reality of the series.

In contrast, *Quantum Leap* (1989–1993), a much more traditional show that premiered just a year before *Twin Peaks*, begins quite differently. While the credits do start with a stylized journey through the clouds, suggesting a kind of "inner" metaphysical space, ultimately they resolve into clips from the show itself, highlighting events, and more specifically the show's premise, rather than a particular space. We see clips taken from episodes of the show, clips of Scott Bakula's character, Sam, waking up in a variety of different bodies. Another traditional series to premiere that year was *Doogie Howser, M.D.* (1989–1993). The credits here similarly focus on setting up the situation rather than the space, beginning with newspaper clippings about the boy genius.

As I did in chapter 3, I want to turn here to several contemporary, post-*Twin Peaks*, show openings, each one highlighting the space of that show in a different way and each one illustrating just how central space has become to today's TV storyworlds.

Justified's setting, for example—Harlan County, Kentucky—shapes both the characters and events in the series. It is the place Raylan Givens must return home to, full of ghosts from his past he must confront. In the opening credits, we see images from the area—a church, a coal processing plant, a gas station—and end with a shot of the county seat taken from a hillside above, the whole storyworld spread out beneath us. Mixed in with these landmark images are those of train tracks, and neighborhood streets—paths, important symbols of movement *into* each episode, but also movement *within* each episode. And as important as the images themselves is the way they are assembled. In many of these clips we seem to be seeing this landscape from the window of a moving car, or perhaps a train. In other words, the credits take us on a kind of tour of the space, further stressing movement, a fact additionally highlighted by the Gangstagrass theme music: "On this lonely road, trying to make it home . . ."

Other recent shows offer a similar opening montage. *True Blood* (2008–2014), for instance, employs virtually the same approach as *Justified*. In this case the camera rises from the Louisiana swamp, connecting us to the show's atmosphere; once we have risen to the point where we have a clear sense of that space, we begin to move through that swamp, then through the Louisiana countryside, town streets, past dilapidated liquor stores and ruined cemeteries. As in the *Justified* credits, the producers here intersperse other images into the visual journey—a striking snake, historical footage of Civil Rights era protests and Ku Klux Klan rallies. But these are ultimately integrated into the overall movement along the path. We are not simply seeing this space in

Figure 4.1. One of the "paths" in *Justified*'s opening credits.
Justified

static images—we are moving through it, *into* it. The sequence becomes more about the area's people as it goes, but it begins with the place that defines those people. The Louisiana landscape tells us exactly what we need to know about who they are, what they believe in, and how they behave.

Another series where space matters is *The Walking Dead*. As we will see in chapter 6, the space of this series matters in part because it is a new space: the civilization of the past has been completely decimated. This, as much as any television world, then, is a brand new reality, one neither we nor the characters really know. We know the place names—Atlanta, Washington, D.C., but those places are no more. What we explore is not the Atlanta that we know today, but rather a hollowed out shell full of walkers and roving gangs of survivors. The series itself is about pushing into these spaces, allowing us to explore this new world. As a result, the characters remain constantly on the move—each refuge they discover ultimately collapses and they must move on to another. The result: we are always moving through this "new" world, learning its rules, exploring it as a world. In fact, the entire plot might be termed "exploratory."

Here again, then, the opening credits have the important job of giving us a sense of this space as well as highlighting the movement that occurs over the course of the series. During this opening we see train tracks and empty roads. We watch walkers in the distance as we travel, again as though *we* are in a car or a train moving through the countryside. And importantly, there are quick shots of maps—maps that remind us of the overall space we inhabit during the show, of what that space once was, and of how we must navigate through it in order to rediscover it.

Figure 4.2. A map featured in *The Walking Dead's* opening credits.
The Walking Dead

We find maps in two other recent show openings, both of which also highlight the world as re-made. In fact, the two opening credit sequences could almost be mistaken for one another. The first accompanies the post-apocalyptic series *The Last Ship* (2014–), in which the world has been decimated by a plague. In the first two seasons, the credits focus on the ship from the series title, the Nathan James, a last remnant of the U.S. Navy that travels the seas in search first for a cure and later for a means of distributing that cure. Interestingly, however, in the most recent season, images of the ship have been replaced by a global map. We watch as a single blue drop falls onto the map, spreading out, turning everything it touches blue, until it encounters areas colored in red that resist it. These images suggest the spread of the cure around the globe and the resistance that cure ultimately meets, a resistance we discover over the course of the third season comes from a militant faction who hope the cure will "purify" the human race. Space here is reduced to a map rather than a series of realistic images of place, but that map offers a powerful sense of how the show relies on space and the question of who controls that space.

The Amazon series, *The Man in the High Castle* uses a map in its opening as well, this one a map of America. As we watch, arrows move across it indicating Nazi takeover of the East Coast and Japanese control over the West. In the first half of the credits we see American landmarks—the Statue of Liberty, Mt. Rushmore—over which images of the enemy invasion appear in shadow—warplanes overhead, paratroopers descending. In the second half of the credits, these American landmarks are replaced by Nazi paraphernalia. Like *The Walking Dead* and *The Last Ship*, *The Man in the High Castle* asks us to enter a world that doesn't really exist—an America that lost World War II and that is now under the joint rule of the Germans and the Japanese. The show's action puts the two coasts in opposition, but also highlights the no-man's- land that lies between them, where the resistance takes shape. The map helps us situate ourselves in the broadest sense in this new reality, letting us know as we enter, not just where it takes place, but what the rules are.

In the opening credits to *House of Cards*, we don't just get a tour of the space—in this case Washington, D.C. We do *get* that tour: we begin at a distance with a wide shot of the city, and soon we are looking out over city streets, neighborhoods that sit in the shadow of the capitol building, statuary, and landmarks. But, as the montage continues, we are also given a sense of how to think about this space. To begin with, our views of D.C. are presented using time lapse photography, suggesting this space as chaotic and always on the move. In addition, as the credits pass, time passes as well, moving us from day to night. As this transition takes place, shadows begin to build up throughout the city. As the sun crosses the sky and begins to set, shadows cover the buildings, offering a sinister symbol of the spread of political corruption, until at last night falls. Yet the rapid pace of the cars through the streets remains even in the darkness, a world of monuments to liberty and freedom turned inside out, ending in a final shot of an upside-down flag and the series title.

Sometimes the "space" of a show can be internal as much as external. Over the course of *The Wire*'s five seasons we investigate Baltimore spaces from the harbor, to the school system, to the newspaper industry—all against the background of the drug trade. These credits treat space somewhat differently from the examples we've seen up to this point though. While we do get quick glimpses of Baltimore—city streets and back alleys, even maps—these are tied together with another important way of conceiving of space—in this case the digital equipment referenced in the title, the "wire" that connects the police to the drug trade they are investigating. While we do travel the streets of Baltimore, we're also given camera shots that follow the surveillance equipment, tracking shots that move along the cords of the equipment, a recognition that the electronics occupy their own space. The effect is to reduce the larger space of the city into a digital, virtual image of that space. In many ways, this is a reflection on the space of the show as postmodern—a reduction of reality to a digital existence, one that exists *inside* the wires.

The same kind of effect occurs in the opening credits to *Mad Men*. The sequence of images hints at the show's New York City setting, but in truth New York City is less important to the series than the office buildings within that city. These are the spaces these characters—and particularly Don Draper, the central figure—inhabit. Thus rather than offer us a tour of the city, these credits provide us with a tour of the office building—though a very particular sort of tour. Rather than moving through hallways and stairwells, we find ourselves falling along with a faceless cutout of a businessman from the top of the building. Here space is shifted vertically, and that space is set up to give us a sense of terror, a feeling that life is out of control. While we end in an office, the fall remains with us as we see the apparently staid image of our man on a couch apparently relaxed and calmly drinking a martini. Ultimately, the credits suggest a deep anxiety toward the space the character inhabits, though that space and the terrors it offers remain hidden beneath (below) a calm exterior.

Three more series—*Sherlock* (2010–), *Wayward Pines* (2015–2016), and *Game of Thrones* (2011–) play with space in an even more postmodern sense. All three draw our attention to the "artificiality" of their landscapes, purposefully reminding us that these worlds are virtual rather than real. All three sets of opening credits highlight this aspect of the series by turning the storyworld into a child's plaything.

In *Sherlock*, the effect is achieved using a tilt-shifted camera. We certainly get a feel for London from these overhead and distant shots of city streets and landmarks, though the movement from image to image grows faster and more chaotic as the credits continue. Yet the camera work gives it all the look of a toy set, an artificial world meant to be played with rather than taken realistically. In fact, this effect sets up the character of Sherlock himself, who is not only intimately connected to the streets of London, but who possesses a kind of omniscient awareness of those streets. We see London through his mind's eye, and in that sense it truly is a plaything. The postmodernism here, then is complex, a recognition that everything exists within Sherlock's mind, that we can't really trust what we see as "real" in the traditional sense. And the show's plot tends to bear this out. *Sherlock*, like *The Wire*, relies heavily on technology. Holmes maintains his connection to the city through text messages and we're frequently shown digital maps in episodes, maps that orient him, but that more importantly help orient us. This space may exist in reality, but it also exists in a very digital form as well, one tied, in this case, to Sherlock's own mind. The space we enter then is doubly virtual—virtual in the sense of being a television series, but virtual as well in the sense that the events occur across digital and mental landscapes.

Rather than tilt shift an actual city, *Wayward Pines*'s opening uses miniature models, including tiny human figures, to show the town's main settings—the hospital, the school, the sheriff's office. Here again, the images remind us of the town's "artificiality." Wayward Pines, as we learn over the course of the first season, is a fake town, an image pretending to be real. While it seems like a sleepy small Idaho town, nestled among the hills, it exists two thousand years in the future, when the rest of the world has fallen to ruin and the world outside the town walls is inhabited by only vaguely humanoid creatures

Figure 4.3. A tilt-shifted image of London streets from above.
Sherlock

who seek to destroy this last remnant of civilization. The façade literally matters because those who learn the truth are inevitably driven to madness, unable to face this truth. But it matters as well because it means that, as with *Sherlock*, every time we enter this world we enter a virtual reality within a virtual reality.

One of the most recognizable opening credit sequences in recent years is that which accompanies the popular series *Game of Thrones*. As much as any contemporary series, space matters here, with the various kingdoms within this space all battling for supremacy. And like *The Last Ship* or *The Man in the High Castle*, the credits use a map to help highlight this fact. The camera pans over the map as it does in these other series' credits, but here the kingdoms on that map are not rendered realistically but rather as a series of clockwork toys, each growing and developing as we watch. The castle at King's Landing rises from the ground; the buildings at Winterfell slide into place; we watch a tiny elevator ascend the northern border wall. Obviously the most important reference here is to the "game" of the title. And yet it is impossible to ignore the way this opening turns the entire space of the show into a child's playland (a move that connects us to our next chapter where we will explore the relationship between television and childhood).

As an end to this analytical exercise, I offer one final set of opening credits, those that accompany the HBO series *The Sopranos*, for they combine many of the techniques we have already examined. Each episode begins in the darkness of a tunnel, from which we emerge, seconds later, into the bright light of the interstate approaching the Jersey Turnpike. We are travelers, invisible passengers alongside Tony Soprano, watching as the world goes by through his windshield, the perfect metaphor for our gaze into the depths of the television screen itself. The sense of motion strikes us before anything else, the lights overhead in the tunnel flickering by, telling us we're headed *somewhere*, even if we may not yet know where. These initial scenes serve several important functions: we're drawn to Tony himself as the center of the story, his presence in the frame, larger than life; meanwhile, the thumping beat of Leonard Cohen's "Woke Up This Morning" sets a swaggering tone, as does the cigar clenched tightly between Tony's teeth and the casual way he grabs his tollbooth ticket. More than anything else, though, this opening credit sequence propels us into the show's physical space: not just New Jersey, but *The Sopranos*' New Jersey, both real and not real. We're shown the landmarks of this space in quick succession—the New York City skyline, the Statue of Liberty, industrial smokestacks, railroad bridges—so there can be no mistake. We also travel *through* it, from its outer edges, through its many small neighborhoods, until at last we reach Tony's home, the very heart of this particular universe. In the space of ninety seconds, the entire world unfolds around us.

To be sure, not all opening credits highlight space in the way these several examples do. *Breaking Bad*, for instance, one of the more important series in television history, offers very little in the way of opening credits: a table of elements and a trail of smoke are all we see here. And while, like *Mad Men* this might be interpreted as a special effect in terms of space, an internal space perhaps, the truth is the show opts to focus more on the events

Figure 4.4. Tony emerges from the tunnel.
The Sopranos

in the episodes themselves—extending the time of those events by cutting the opening credits and using this ten second credit sequence as little more than a placeholder. The same is true of *Girls*—which uses only a title placard in different colors each week—and for *Lost* and *The Closer*.

And, as I mention above, with the increase in our use of streaming services, we don't need to be reintroduced to a show's world over and over again because we never really leave it. Only when we walk away from it for some amount of time do we need to re-enter it. Does this mean opening credit sequences may ultimately lose importance over the long term? I cannot say for certain, but I doubt it. While binge watching will inevitably increase as time goes on, we will likely never reach a point where we only watch shows in their entirety, all in one sitting. As long as we must stop and return, credit sequences will have an important role to play in moving us into the storyworld.

Chapter 5

"Can You Tell Me How to Get, How to Get to Sesame Street?"

Kid's TV and Imaginary Spaces

Each series we choose to watch is a new beginning for us, with a first episode—a pilot—that invites us into a new space. As I argued in chapter 4, each episode of that series restarts our journey into that world, re-creating the space for us, inviting us to re-enter the virtual reality.

These beginnings can be very personal for us. We choose which spaces we want to experience; we choose whether or not to return to that space, a decision that connects to how we feel about that space—whether it feels realistic, believable, or comfortable. We may not feel the same way about *The Sopranos*' world as our partner does; we may like visiting *The Office*, while a coworker finds it claustrophobic; maybe *True Blood* feels like home, or maybe we like it because it doesn't, because it feels like an escape from what we know.

Television begins for us in another very personal way: for each of us there is a first show, a first exposure to television as a space we might inhabit, as a place where we belong. Often that place feels private. *Sesame Street*, *Dora the Explorer*, *Barney*: these aren't just our first acquaintance with the medium; they are storyworlds aimed specifically at us. Parents might sit in the room and monitor what we do—good parents might discuss with us what we watch—but they aren't engaged in these worlds in the way we are. Cookie Monster doesn't speak to our dad the way he talks to us when we are four. And for a time we don't recognize that mom and dad have their own relationships to the television, their own storyworlds they enjoy. Books and stories may offer a similar experience for us when we're young, but those experiences are filtered through the adults who read or tell them to us. TV, in contrast, speaks to us directly; we access it on our own. In the beginning, these places seem like a secret, places no one knows about but us, like an imaginary friend, or a whispered game of make-believe we act out in private with our stuffed toys.

These shows—children's shows—teach us. They teach us how to read, how to count, how to get along with others. But more than this, they teach us how to participate in an imagined TV "reality." *Mr. Rogers' Neighborhood* doesn't just introduce us to its own world; it shows us how to access all television worlds—how they function, how to move inside them, what place they should hold in relation to our "real" lives.

We might, of course, view this sort of "education" in a sinister light. To return to my discussion of Plato in chapter 1, who are more "innocent" and susceptible to a virtual world's lure than children? In fact, the arguments against exposing children to television date back as far as television itself. Initially, these arguments mainly revolved around television violence, leading to thousands of research studies and, as early as 1952, even congressional inquiries (Hoerner 1999). In more recent years, a host of additional arguments have been lodged, not just against children watching television, but specifically against "children's television," from generalized fears that TV will "rot your brain" to arguments about advertising during children's programming, to complaints that many kids series reinforce gender biases.

While I feel it important to acknowledge these many arguments (and I am certain I am only scratching the surface of the many arguments that have been made), I do not wish to become bogged down debating the relative merits of each one. As this cursory list of topics suggests, you can find whole libraries full of books and articles on the subject. My goal here is of a somewhat different nature. Specifically, I'm less interested in parsing the positive and negative aspects of television than in thinking about what it can do and exploring how it goes about doing it. Television is about living in alternative spaces; this chapter deals with just how the medium teaches us, from our youngest days, to do this.

A BRIEF HISTORY OF CHILDREN'S TV

Like soap operas, children's television is almost as old as television itself, and like soap operas, it seems to have been among the first TV programming to make full use of the medium's strengths. Like soaps, for instance, many of these shows weren't merely broadcast serially, but daily, making them a part of kids' everyday lives. "What time is it kids?" *The Howdy Doody Show* (1946–1957) asked every weekday for thirteen years: "It's Howdy Doody time!" And *Howdy Doody* didn't just understand the importance of time to television, but space as well. Buffalo Bill came to us from a well-defined location, where "all those kids in the peanut gallery" served as stand-ins for the millions watching at home. The theme song defined this space as well: "Let's give a rousing cheer, 'Cause Howdy Doody's here," the children sang. Howdy Doody was "here," with us, with you, in the virtual world of the show. And the show was, after all, its own world: during the credits a map of the United States would appear and there, in the middle, marked in bold letters, was the town of Doodyville, complete with landmarks like Cobb's General Store or the Triple B Ranch. Sometimes we might leave Doodyville entirely and head into the country of "Early Tibet." Other times a character might be out in the world and we'd follow his adventures through the magic of the kinescope. These trips away from the town though only helped reinforce the reality of Doodyville as a place: only a real space can be left; only a real space can be returned to.

The Howdy Doody Show, in fact, became an important model for children's television, especially in terms of its structure. Any single episode might contain several different narratives—a story about one of the town's characters, a kinescope film of Clarabell the clown on a farm, a silent film narrated by Buffalo Bob, an adventure with the Rice Krispies' Snap, Crackle, and Pop—but we always returned to Doodyville and the Peanut Gallery, a kind of home base or spatial center.

Captain Kangaroo (1955–1984), starring Bob Keeshan (who had played Clarabell the Clown on *The Howdy Doody Show*) utilized a similar structure and developed its space in a similar fashion. Episodes always took place in the Treasure House, the Captain's Place—another spatial center. Early episodes began with the Captain opening a miniature door, inviting us into the space of the Treasure House. In later seasons, the opening was animated, and we followed the Captain as he arrived at the House, a ring of keys in his hand, to open the door and invite us into this storyworld. Like *The Howdy Doody Show*, an episode was usually filled with several smaller narratives—cartoons, stories from the Captain himself, visits from celebrity guests—but everything ultimately happened within the many rooms of the single house. Soupy Sales's 1950s kids' shows (which were produced under a variety of different titles) took place in the unified space of a single room; visitors would show up at the door and windows, reminding us of the larger world outside this space. In the 1960s Bozo the Clown rose in popularity, franchised on a number of local stations around the country, and utilizing the same basic format as these earlier programs, with Bozo introducing cartoon segments and playing games with kids in the studio. In this case, home base was a big top circus.

Other early children's programming enlarged the space of the show, but the space always mattered. *Disney's Wonderful World of Color*'s title declared it a storyworld space so vast it might literally be thought of as a "world." Each week featured a new film, but the series title helped hold all of the content together in a single imaginative story universe. *The Flintstones* and *The Jetsons* resituated children to a completely other time—the Stone Age and the future—but the temporal shift essentially only served to offer children a whole new landscape to explore. A big part of the humor in both shows—as in early sitcoms such as *Green Acres*—were the quirks of those spaces: Wilma's pelican dishwasher, Barney's dinosaur lawnmower, Elroy's television wristwatch.

Much of the more recent children's television programming has followed the patterns set by the first shows. *Pee-Wee's Playhouse* (1986–1991) for instance follows the *Howdy Doody/Captain Kangaroo* model, setting all the events within a single house. The opening credits work deictically: we begin in a kind of jungle forest and we move through this space, along a path, until we arrive at the playhouse itself. There we follow Pee-Wee inside, much as we did Captain Kangaroo. Once inside, the lyrics become about the playhouse itself: Pee-Wee rushes about the space as the theme music describes its various entertainments—the magic screen, Globey the world globe, Jambi the Genii, and the puppetland band. *Fraggle Rock* (1983–1987), *Blue's Clues* (1996–2007), *Spongebob Squarepants* (1999–2018), *Lazytown* (2002–2016), *Barney & Friends* (1992–2009)—all of these take place in clearly defined spaces as well.

PBS's *Arthur* (1996–) takes place in Elwood City, but more interesting than *Arthur* is its spinoff series, *Postcards from Buster* (2004–). As a spinoff, the show automatically expands the space of the original series, but additionally *Buster*'s format emphasizes movement, defining Ellwood as "home" at the same time it pushes into new spaces each week. The premise of the show has Buster, a rabbit who is Arthur's best friend in the original series, traveling on vacation around the country with his family. Buster visits a variety of locations, each episode featuring a different lifestyle associated with a different space: in one episode he spends time with a farm family; in one he learns about the Lakota in South Dakota; in another he finds out about hip hop culture. In each case Buster narrates a short video diary of life in that particular place.

Thomas and Friends involves movement as well. Thomas the Tank Engine and his railroad companions roam about on rail lines, constantly pushing into new spaces. Their movement allows us not merely to exist in a virtual space but to move about in that space, to explore it. In the same general way, Bob and his construction friends in *Bob the Builder* (1998–) move about the town of Bobsville (later Sunflower Valley and Fixham Harbor), uncovering many interconnected neighborhoods. In addition, Bob is—as the title makes clear—about building within this town. As a result, the show becomes not merely about inhabiting a space or even moving through that space, but actually creating that space. Finally, *Dora the Explorer* offers a particularly strong example of character movement. In this case the show is designed to visit a new location each episode. Dora and her friends identify a destination, use a map to pinpoint that destination and identify the path to get there, develop a set of landmarks that will guide them on their way, and then make the trip one landmark at a time.

All of these shows teach children important lessons about "exploring" their own worlds—the value of multicultural encounters, how to improve your community, what it means to plan an adventure. But on a deeper, more fundamental level, they also teach important lessons about how to navigate imaginative storyworlds: how characters are defined; how stories are structured; and strategies for engaging with virtual spaces.

PLAY AND REALITY

Child psychologist D. W. Winnicott argued in the 1960s and 1970s that art—especially narrative—begins in childhood. Childhood is when we as humans first develop a need for a virtual space, a storyworld that exists in a place related to reality but located just outside that reality. Winnicott posited a developmental process in infants that involves "transitional objects," objects that take on magical significance for a child. A newborn begins life with an understanding of the world as absolutely and totally subjective. She views everything around her as a part of her self. The transitional object works to introduce her to objectivity, the concept that a world exists outside of her own individual reality. As Winnicott describes it,

"In common experience one of the following occurs, complicating autoerotic experience such as thumb sucking:

> (i) with the other hand the baby takes an external object, say a part of a sheet or blanket, into the mouth along with the fingers;
> (ii) somehow or other the bit of cloth is held and sucked, or not actually sucked; the objects used naturally include napkins and (later) handkerchiefs, and this depends on what is readily and reliably available; or
> (iii) the baby starts from early months to pluck wool and to collect it and to use it for the caressing part of the activity; less commonly, the wool is swallowed, even causing trouble." (2005, 3–4)

While it is in the mouth, the external object works subjectively: the blanket or toy is literally inside the child, a part of her self. When the blanket or other object is removed, however, its removal alerts the child to the fact that a separate reality exists outside her own body.

This is an important and necessary lesson in childhood development, but beyond teaching children about objective reality, the process leaves a significant residue in a child's psyche. In fact, the "transitional object" doesn't simply become part of objective reality for the infant. Rather, because of its transitional nature—because it once *was* part of the child's self, it participates in both of her realities—the subjective and the objective. The transitional object becomes liminal: it occupies an in-between space of "play" and "imagination," an "intermediate area between the subjective and that which is objectively perceived" (3). Such objects and intermediate spaces develop as the child develops: "Patterns set in infancy may persist into childhood, so that the original soft object continues to be absolutely necessary at bedtime or at times of loneliness or when a depressed mood threatens" (4). As a result, we need these objects, these spaces; they allow us to develop a healthy relationship to the world. They serve as mediators between us and the world, allowing us to test our ideas and behaviors in relative safety.

Further, Winnicott speculates that such liminal childhood spaces are ultimately the root of all art, the foundation of "play, and of artistic creativity and appreciation, and of religious feeling, and of dreaming, and also of fetishism, lying and stealing, the origin of loss and of affectionate feeling, drug addiction, the talisman of obsessional rituals, etc." (5). We cling to these spaces in childhood; we cling to them as well in adulthood, and Winnicott seems to suggest that when we don't employ them in healthy ways—in art, for instance—they may manifest in much more unhealthy activities.

Winnicott does not specifically mention narrative here, yet his comment implies a space like a storyworld where play might occur. The very function of narrative in such a formulation is to give us, as adult humans, a place to try on, as it were, various play clothes, to experiences events different from our everyday lives, to learn without having to absolutely commit to changing who we are. And so, we do experience these worlds as in-between spaces, places where we may become attached to Harry Potter, or Quinton Compson, or Ishmael, may cry with them or laugh, may miss them when they are gone. We recognize that ultimately they only exist in a virtual sense; we know we can step away, see them objectively as part of a story, even think about the ways in which a story is constructed, or what the story might suggest about our "real" existence. The objects and spaces are not mere symbols, though, however much we may be able to view them with objectivity. Importantly, Winnicott draws a distinction between symbolism and the transitional objects that interest him:

> When symbolism is employed the infant is already clearly distinguishing between fantasy and fact, between inner objects and external objects, between primary creativity and perception. But the term transitional object, according to

> my suggestion, gives room for the process of becoming able to accept difference and similarity. (6)

The distinction he draws here argues that the transitional object is experiential—it opens up "room," an alternate reality, a space in which we experience imagined worlds subjectively.

In the early 1990s, philosopher Kendall Walton developed a similar conception of play as the root of art, and like Winnicott posited a liminal space in which that play occurs. While his approach is less based in empirical psychology, it amounts to the same essential idea. Walton introduces the phrase "make-believe" to identify the spaces we inhabit during play and—like Winnicott—argues that the origins of make-believe and play ultimately extend out into our adult lives in the form of artistic expression: "In order to understand paintings, plays, films, and novels, we must first look at dolls, hobbyhorses, toy trucks, and teddy bears. The activities in which representational works of art are embedded and which give them their point are best seen as continuous with children's games of make-believe" (1993, 11).

Since the advent of television, children's programming has become an important version of that same imaginary space, that land of make-believe. *Pee-Wee's Playhouse* and *Dora the Explorer* teach us many important lessons, but always by allowing us to experience those lessons in a safe space, a virtual reality where we can come to no real harm. In an episode of *Barney*, for example ("Trading Places"), BJ, one of Barney's young dinosaur friends, feels jealous that his younger sister Baby Bop doesn't have chores the way he does. When the two switch roles for a day, he experiences humiliation at being treated like a baby. In watching the episode, we learn that lesson as well. In learning it we may experience real emotions—jealousy and shame—and these may have real impacts on our behavior in the "real" world. In the end, however, the experience happens at one remove from reality, in a play space, and we learn the lesson without harm to our selves.

But because we come to such television spaces so early in our lives, they not only *are* that space. As one of our first organized exposures to such spaces they teach us generally how to *use* that space. Mother Goose rhymes, or Little Golden Books work similarly, training children to understand oral and textual narrative: kids learn through repetition and formulas how a text should work. In fact, the *Deixis in Narrative* workgroup argues in "Preschool Children's Introduction of Character into Their Oral Stories: Evidence for Deictic Organization of First Narratives" (Duchan 1994) that children as young as four have already absorbed the essentials of narrative. In the same way, *Sesame Street* trains them to enter the narrative of the television space, how to think about it, but also how to use it.

AN EDUCATION IN STORYWORLD SPACES

In the remainder of this chapter I focus my analysis on three specific shows: *Sesame Street*, *Mr. Rogers' Neighborhood*, and *Teletubbies*. Each of these series has had great success in terms of audience numbers, suggesting their wide influence on children and ultimately childhood development. They've also garnered multiple awards, both from television organizations and educational institutions. Each contains elements common to children's television, elements I've already touched on in relation to programs like *The Howdy Doody Show* and *Pee-Wee's Playhouse*, so they work well as illustrations of children's TV's general structures. All three also have the advantage of being deliberately and obviously educationally oriented, which might help to ameliorate some hesitancy about connecting children to television. Finally, though, each does more than perhaps any other kids series, both to introduce children to the show's spatial qualities and to teach children how to recognize and experience those qualities in the televisual world.

By any measure *Sesame Street* is among the most popular, if not the most popular, children's television show in history. It has been on the air continuously since 1969—almost fifty years, an eternity in television time. A 1996 survey found that over 95 percent of preschoolers had watched the show by the time they were three years old, and a 2006 survey found that 77 million adults had watched the program at some point in their lives. It has won 167 Emmy Awards. In total the show has filmed nearly 4,500 episodes, more than any American series outside news-oriented programs and soap operas.

The name "Sesame Street" immediately draws attention to the show's spatial qualities, encouraging children to think of it as a specific location. The logo is a street sign. The theme song emphasizes the spatial element as well, the idea of traveling to the location, following a path into the storyworld: "I'm on my way to where the air is sweet," the lyrics tell us. The second verse mentions "neighbors," suggesting a neighborhood and a place "where we meet." And the various opening credit sequences that have accompanied the show through the years play on this idea of moving into a space as well. The earliest version, from 1969, features children moving—kids walking and running, a little girl riding a tricycle, a child sitting on a tractor, another going down a slide, older children roller skating—all apparently heading somewhere, ostensibly, as the song goes, "on [their] way" to Sesame Street. Later versions of the credits play on the same basic theme of movement into a storyworld. For example, season 39's opening features kids and many of the show's characters all traveling in various kinds of vehicles, animated in this case—cars, a hot air balloon, a city bus, another tricycle—all heading into this storyworld.

In many ways the show follows the format set up by *The Howdy Doody Show*. That is, it works almost like a variety show, with short films, cartoons, and skits all incorporated into the larger context of a whole episode. Even more than its forebears, though, *Sesame Street* from the beginning worked to unify its various elements. So, for example, a single episode might focus on cooking, or cheering for something, or how to make a new friend. Each of the various components throughout an episode work together to emphasize that single idea. We don't just return to Sesame Street as home base—we return again and again to the same themes. This helps provide additional unity to the show in terms of content, but it also helps unify the viewers' sense of Sesame Street as a single location. And *Sesame Street* always begins on the street itself, with Big Bird, or Oscar, or Elmo, so that wherever the action may lead us, ultimately it remains grounded in that one location, that single street with its tenement building, stoop, and newsstand.

Similarly, *Mr. Rogers' Neighborhood* clearly understands television and itself as a virtual space, and while it ultimately has kids' best interests at heart, takes full advantage of TV's world-making power to draw them into

Figure 5.1. Big Bird invites children to follow him to Sesame Street during the show's opening credits.
***Sesame Street*, season 32**

that space. Here again, for example, the name of the show itself references a specific place, a neighborhood. We begin each episode, in the opening credits, by traveling through that space—a child's model of neighborhood streets featuring houses, businesses, the local school—finally arriving at Mr. Rogers's house itself. Mr. Rogers arrives through the front door, or sometimes we see him (like Captain Kangaroo), arrive from outside and open the door with his key. His song reminds us, "It's a beautiful day in the *neighborhood*, a beautiful day for a *neighbor*" (emphasis added). In addition, as with *Sesame Street*, there are various segments in any single *Mr. Rogers'* episodes but all those pieces fit together to offer a unified theme. In fact, *Mr. Rogers* frequently offers week-long themes on subjects from manufacturing, to divorce, to being brave. The week of ideas always comes back to the single space—a space Mr. Rogers carefully enters at the beginning and exits at the end of each episode.

But if these two series are more educational than most, they also do more than most to teach children about television itself and more broadly about the nature of storyworlds.

Sesame Street, for instance, understands its own place in the broader TV landscape and works to imitate that landscape. In particular, it mimics the "flow" of TV programming. That is, an episode consists of shorter programming, brief clips all bound up together. Further *Sesame Street*'s flow includes many standard TV tropes. For example, an episode might move smoothly from a live action story involving Grover, to a commercial for the letter "T," to a news report from Kermit the Frog, to a short documentary on kids learning Spanish in an after-school program, in the same way a typical night of "adult" television programming moves from a sitcom like *Modern Family*, into commercials for hair care products, potato chips, and dog leashes, through a news teaser, an ad for another show on ABC, and back into the show again. Each piece of this stream of content works as its own sort of virtual space, but together they turn the whole of TV content into one large space. Through its mimicry of this stream *Sesame Street* gives kids practice in navigating what might otherwise be a confusing tangle of media images.

In addition, the show highlights television watching by having characters watch TV themselves. That is the characters in this storyworld space enter their own storyworld spaces as well, modeling how we should treat such spaces. The most important character in this regard is Elmo, who has his own "show" within the larger context of *Sesame Street*, not coincidentally called "Elmo's *World*" (emphasis added). Many of the elements in this world are screen based, including the Mr. Noodle segment, where kids try to help a bumbling Mr. Noodle figure out the idea or object of the day. Mr. Noodle seems to exist inside a window, hidden beneath a yellow window-shade, but when the shade is raised so we can watch his antics, the window seems remarkably like a television screen. Even more pronounced, Elmo often watches a "channel" on his television to learn more about the day's topic.

The end result of *Sesame Street*'s structure is an emphasis not merely on itself as a virtual reality but on all television programming as virtual reality. Offering a "flow," of programming, situates children within the broader context of television as a medium, illustrating for kids episode by episode how that flow of images work, introducing them to the medium's central attributes. And *Sesame Street* goes even further, frequently using parodies of existing "adult" shows. In addition to Kermit the Frog's news reports on events such as the rescue of Rapunzel, an episode might include a *House of Cards* spoof that tells the story of the three little pigs, or an *Orange Is the New Black* parody dealing with healthy eating habits. These skits remind kids of the broader world of television beyond their own viewing and help prepare them for that wider world.

At the same time it understands its position as virtual reality, though, *Sesame Street* also understands its role as "transitional object." In particular, the series works hard to mix its imaginative elements with its realistic elements, setting up a kind of middle ground between subjectivity and objectivity, a space in which the viewer can play. Part of this has to do with the mix of programming—the objective reality of a live-action film, for example, juxtaposed against the imaginary world of a cartoon. In addition, the show mixes real human characters with puppets, suggesting adults too possess the capacity for moving easily in and out of an imagined reality.

Mr. Rogers' Neighborhood mixes the real and the fictional to an even greater extent, with Mr. Rogers offering multiple levels of "reality," to his young viewers and helping them move fluidly and wisely between them. Nancy Curry, one of Mr. Rogers's former colleagues, points out that he was quite aware of Winnicott's work and the importance of make-believe spaces:

> The importance of pretend play and reality is at the heart of Fred Rogers' work. Daily he invites children to enter play space, and together they confront both the inner reality of imagination and the shared reality of the world that Winnicott so poetically describes. As a classmate, colleague, and observer of Fred Rogers, I have been "Fred-watching" for nearly three decades. In that time, I have come to understand why his blend of reality and fantasy is so important in a child's development and how his program aids in the vital developmental task of resolving subjective and objective reality. (1996)

A good deal of this work has to do with the layers of reality Mr. Rogers creates. In one sense, Mr. Rogers is the adult, who comes to the play space of the neighborhood from his adult job, demonstrating how all humans—even "big people"—can and should be capable of moving easily between "reality" and "imagination." Like *Sesame Street*, the *Mr. Rogers' Neighborhood*'s studio set is highly stylized—that is, it is designed to represent a "real" home, but at the same time the elements in the house are obviously sets—the flimsy walls and doors, the plastic trees outside the windows, the over-acting Mr. McFeely, the mailman, all point up the fact that this is a television space, a safe place to play with ideas. Mr. Rogers wants children to see the seams. But in a way even more deliberate than *Sesame Street*, he helps differentiate each level. This is especially true with the "Land of Make-Believe" that he incorporates into every episode. An episode might begin with an object Mr. Rogers brings into the play space—a crayon, for example. Mr. Rogers demonstrates how to use the crayon and talks about the importance of imagination and the freedom to be found through creativity. Then he shows a film clip of a Crayola Crayon factory, talking us gently through each aspect of the crayon making process. But once he has established this object and taught lessons about it in "reality," he allows us to move into the "Land of Make-Believe" and think through what we've learned from a subjective, imaginative perspective. We travel into another world, where King Friday sponsors an art competition, and the various other characters—Lady Elaine, Daniel Tiger—consider what they might like to create.

Mr. Rogers understood his show's place in the television landscape, and never tried to pretend his show was disconnected from that landscape. So, for example, in the crayon episode the film clip he shows appears on a wall-mounted screen that seems very much like a TV. And we enter the land of make-believe on a trolley, a path from one level of reality to another. But Mr. Rogers carefully peaks behind the screens he sets up. Another Mr. Rogers scholar, George Gerbner, writes about an episode where Mr. Rogers visits the set of the TV show, *The Incredible Hulk*.

> In one episode (one of many examples), he goes behind the scenes of a scary television show, *The Incredible Hulk*. He shows all of us how this is made. In a single stroke he achieves the shift from attribution to inference. "Attribution" is a kind of childish way of looking at a story as something natural arising out of the natural world—in other words, attributing meaning to something that's merely an image. "Inference" is when you can get behind the scenes and know there is a script, an actor, a camera, and make-up. Infer from what you see and you are in control. And as soon as you do that, it becomes an enriching experience no matter how bad the program may be. Rogers allows a young audience to make this crucial shift. (1996)

Herein lies the exceptional nature of programs like *Sesame Street* and *Mr. Rogers' Neighborhood*. It is true, for example, that *The Howdy Doody Show* in 1947, offered kids an experiential "flow" of images just like these later shows. But that flow was based on attribution rather than inference: Buffalo

Bob moved us seamlessly from a film on the kinescope to a skit on set, to a commercial for Colgate. But the commercial was real, meaning a child might easily see the advertising as part of the fun and invest in it without parsing the differences between show and shilling.

Sesame Street, in contrast, uses "commercials" for educational purposes, promoting letters and numbers as opposed to toothpaste: "Mrs. Wilkins wouldn't you like a letter W?" a small orange cartoon man asks a woman in pink in a cartoon scene. "The Letter W is wonderful," he goes on, "With the new, improved letter W you can have windows, watches, walls, and water buffalo." The result: kids learn to *use* television rather than allowing it to use them. *Mr. Rogers' Neighborhood* goes even further, teaching children directly about the importance of imagination and even TV's place within imagination and creativity, but always explaining to them very clearly how it might be used.

Finally, I end here by looking at a less traditional children's television show, but one that is no less popular than the two we have already examined: *Teletubbies* (1997–2001). Here again, the show certainly understands the importance of space. It takes place in "Teletubby Land," and while the teletubbies may have any number of adventures in an episode, the show makes sure we see the land in which those adventures take place as a unified whole, a home base. The show moves us deictically into the space at the beginning of each episode: "One day, in Teletubby Land. . ." Like *Mr. Rogers' Neighborhood*, *Teletubbies* promotes a clear understanding of television space as an imaginative artistic space—in Winnicott's terms as a liminal space where children can participate in make-believe. Teletubby Land offers bright, inviting colors and characters that are especially palatable to young children, characters who, because of the way they talk and behave, work as perfect stand-ins for the audience watching them. The show begins and ends with the rising and setting of the "Sunshine Baby," who watches over everything that happens in Teletubby Land, and who serves as a metaphor for the children at home who watch over what happens as well. This sun provides the "god's-eye" perspective on this world to contrast the actions of the tubbies themselves.

And like *Sesame Street* and *Mr. Rogers' Neighborhood*, *Teleubbies* understands its role as a television show for children: part of its job is to help children make sense of TV. The very title of the show draws our attention to this fact. The emphasis here isn't on a street or a neighborhood. Instead it is on television itself: the "tele" of teletubbies refers to the screens in the creatures' bellies and the receiving antennas on their heads. At some point during each episode, the tubbies get together to receive a broadcast signal. One of them does and the others congratulate him and gather round to watch the broadcast. What else does all of this suggest but a privileging of television, a sense of television's central importance in our lives. Furthermore, the broadcast appears essentially inside the teletubby, suggesting we should internalize, take in subjectively, what we see on the screen.

In contrast to these other series, though, the teletubbies' world is more obviously artificial: the tubbies live in a futuristic looking bubble. They eat tubby toast—obviously plastic. They roam about on grass that is far too green to be real. They themselves are unrealistic creatures. And no actual humans appear in the series with one exception. That exception is the various real life children and adults who appear in the live-action film clips. The result: the tubbies themselves—what we're watching—are clearly artificial, while "television"—what the tubbies themselves watch—represents the real.

The teletubbies offer "postmodern TV," a particular flavor of television space we will explore in greater depth in chapter 8. For now, it is enough to say that the show recognizes it is a show, and it makes no bones about letting the children who watch it know it is a show. At the same time, it manages to fuse the storyworld with reality by filtering both through the screen of the television. This isn't quite what Fred Rogers had in mind when he sought to create a series that would teach children how to handle transitional objects and virtual spaces. Yet it also doesn't seem unreasonable to suggest the

Figure 5.2. La La receives a TV broadcast signal.
Teletubbies

Teletubbies might be the *Mr. Rogers' Neighborhood* of the twenty-first century, a liminal television space designed to teach children about the larger liminal space of television by making obvious its own artistic mechanisms.

Chapter 6

"To Boldly Go Where No One Has Gone Before"

Reinventing the World

If television is, as I have argued, about building worlds, then science fiction and especially post-apocalyptic series offer the most extreme example of this process in action. Because they take us to another place and/or time, other from our own, a science fiction series necessarily begins from nothing. When we encounter a science fiction storyworld, we must go through a process of learning that space and the rules that govern it. This is even truer for a post-apocalyptic narrative, which requires not only that we learn how the world operates, but that we participate with the characters in building, or rather rebuilding it. In short, if we want to understand how a television program *creates* an inhabitable virtual reality, these genres offer us the best place from which to begin, the clearest illustration of how TV series, in general, operate.

SCIENCE FICTION WORLDS

While it has sometimes been dismissed as "merely" genre fiction—or worse a kind of "trash" literature—science fiction actually offers an important analogue for art, in general, and narrative storyworlds, in particular. "Science fiction" can be a difficult term to define (the *Encyclopedia of Science Fiction* suggests "There is really no good reason to expect a workable definition of sf will ever be established" (2017)), but critic Darko Suvin's 1972 definition offers one starting point. Suvin writes of science fiction as "a literary genre whose necessary and sufficient conditions are the presence of and interaction of estrangement and cognition, and whose main formal device is an imaginative framework alternative to the author's empirical environment" (2016, 8–9). The most striking aspect of this definition is that it might be applied to essentially any narrative work. By the "interaction of estrangement and cognition" Suvin seems to mean a "mental shift" from one space to another, or from the "empirical environment"—real life—to an "imaginative alternative framework." In Suvin's formulation, then, science fiction "transports" us from the here and now into a virtual reality distinct from our own. This seems remarkably similar to David Herman's explanation of the "storyworld" and its "ability to transport interpreters from the here and now of face-to-face interaction, or the space-time coordinates of an encounter with printed text or cinematic narrative, to the here and now that constitute the deictic center of the world being told about," which we encountered in chapter 1. Both definitions involve moving from the space of the "here and now" into another "imaginative" or virtual space.

In *Science Fiction*, Patrick Parrinder points out that "In many cases the knowledge offered by science fiction takes the tangible form of ideas; the genre has been widely regarded as a 'literature of ideas,' especially political and scientific ones" (1981, 43). He goes on to quote T. A. Shippey, whose "The Cold War in Science Fiction" argues that the genre often provides "a cover, or a frame, for discussion of many real issues [. . .] issues such as the nature of science, the conflict of business and government, the limits of loyalty, the power of social norms to affect individual perception" (43–44). Keith Booker makes a similar point about dystopian fiction, a near relative to science fiction: "the treatment of imaginary societies in the best dystopian fiction is always highly relevant more or less directly to specific 'realworld' societies and issues" (1994, 19). What these scholars suggest is that science fiction allows us to better reflect on the important social issues of our own time and space by relocating us to another time and space. The "cover" of that new, imagined environment gives us the freedom to explore these often thorny or controversial subjects without necessarily confronting them directly.

These formulations connect us to the idea of a liminal space as developed by Winnicott and Walton. That is, by placing us in an imagined space, one that resembles our own but that is distinct enough from it to allow us critical distance, we inhabit that place where Winnicott suggests we work things out in play. It is the middle ground between subjectivity and objectivity—the subjective involvement in another world combined with the objective criticism of our own world.

But again, while science fiction does this in an extreme sense, we might ultimately attribute this affect to "narrative" broadly conceived and not just to "science fiction." A Dickens novel, for instance, might give us a tragic view of life on the London streets of Victorian England, but as a fiction it exists as one removed from reality; we might weep for the children we find there—and Dickens hopes we will—but we are not quite as emotionally devastated as we might be were we to encounter them in real life. Seen in this light, science fiction offers a kind of blueprint for thinking about art and fiction generally. All storyworlds remove us to some point outside reality; science fiction just does so in a more obvious, self-conscious way.

Television science fiction accomplishes this task no less than traditional text-based science fiction, and often in many of the same ways. Such series create a space and encourage us to move through that space, building worlds as they go. *The Twilight Zone* (1959–1964) emphasizes space in its various opening monologue versions: "You are travelling through another dimension"; "It is the middle ground between light and shadow"; "You unlock this door with the key of imagination." And Gene Roddenberry's famous formulation of *Star Trek* as "*Wagon Train* to the stars," reminds us that both series focused on moving us into unchartered territory, discovering new spaces, expanding their own storyworld boundaries.

The Twilight Zone and the original *Star Trek* exist in a time when most television programs were still episodic. That is, any given episode might make a strong point about racism or war, or friendship, but the point was contained in that single episode. By the next episode the show would have moved on to a completely new issue. One of the most powerful recent science fiction series is SyFy Channel's reboot of the late 1970s classic, *Battlestar Galactica.* The series arrived on the heels of 9/11, when America had become mired in the Iraq War and was just beginning to learn about our government's use of "enhanced interrogation techniques," and black sites. *Battlestar* mined that particular time period for much of its content. As with most forms of science fiction, it situated us in another time and place in order to confront serious social and cultural issues from a safe space. Unlike most science fiction though, because it took the form of a television series, it could use its seriality to look at the entire war on terror, raising a whole series of questions and from numerous perspectives. Early on the questions are relatively simple: the power struggle between President Laura Roslin and Admiral William Adama takes center stage, as the two debate what balance a government under attack should strike between its military and civilian responsibilities. By the third episode, the show was confronting another issue, one connected to prisoner detainment in Guantanamo Bay: what happens to prisoners in the case of an apparently interminable war? As it evolved *Battlestar* considered such topics as the morality and effectiveness of torture, the psychological and emotional consequences of endless war, and the dangers of seeing the enemy as "pure evil."

In addition to taking advantage of its seriality to explore themes in depth, *Battlestar* also pushed against its spatial boundaries in a quite literal sense. Again, science fiction typically requires its viewer learn to navigate a new location, but *Battlestar* highlights this element. In the first scene of the introductory mini-series we have no frame of reference. We find ourselves on a small space station, an outpost, where a bored-seeming, middle-aged man enters a formally decorated room containing only one piece of furniture—a table in the middle. He walks to the table, situates himself and waits for what he thinks will be another yearly no-show from the cylons, a "race" of robots with whom humanity negotiated a peace some forty years ago. This diplomatic meeting was set up to safeguard the peace, but the cylons haven't been seen in some thirty years. Unexpectedly, however, the door at the other end of the room does open and a blonde woman steps in, flanked by two imposing looking cylons. The blonde woman delivers a cryptic speech, she approaches the man and kisses him. With that the space station explodes. From the beginning, then, we are put off balance: we struggle to figure out what's happening in this scene, why the cylons have suddenly reappeared, why the blonde woman is with them, just what it is she's telling this man; but then in an instant anything we may have worked out from the few clues we've been given is destroyed. This world, in short, is a blank canvas.

This moment, though, is only a metaphor, a first strike in a larger genocide that occurs. The cylons essentially destroy the twelve human home worlds in the first two-part mini-series, leaving less than 60,000 humans still alive on a handful of transport ships and one battleship. We, along with the characters, are set adrift. The space they knew is gone, and they must push into unknown spaces if they are to survive. The series then doesn't simply drop us into a new space; it forces the characters to explore a new space as well, allowing us to inhabit their perspective as they do so, to feel their disorientation but also the knowledge they gain as their journey continues. In short, the series performs for us the act of entering a new space; it is a television series whose plot enacts the process of watching a television series.

To some extent, the series makes a habit of keeping us, along with the characters, in the dark. In the earliest episodes the humans are relentlessly pursued by the cylons, and must frantically jump almost at random through hyperspace in their attempt to escape. The effect is disorienting, complicating our understanding of the show's space, perpetually limiting what we can know about this space. At the same time, these early episodes set up an important piece of dramatic irony: we know the cylons now look like humans, that there are many copies, and that they have managed to infiltrate the fleet. This too, keeps us off balance. Besides the unsettling effect of dramatic irony itself, we know who some of the infiltrators are, but not all, and are left wondering—until the final season, in fact—who the others might be.

Yet *Battlestar* isn't simply about disorienting us within its spaces—such a series might be intriguing for an audience at first, but eventually we would tire of having no center. Instead, the show is about pushing us to explore a space, allowing us to understand it a piece at a time, and promising us a "home"—Earth—in the end. One of the important ways *Battlestar* captures this dual sense of feeling lost and finding our way is by alternating between the "tour" and the "god's-eye view." That first scene, in which the space station is destroyed, sets up this alternation. We begin with one man's view, one man's confusion about what is happening. The kiss the woman gives him is entirely personal. But as the station explodes, as the ashes are fading into the darkness of space, the camera pulls back to reveal a massive cylon ship: we move from an individual perspective to one that takes in the entire situation.

The following scenes, which introduce us to the series' primary space and most of its characters works similarly. To begin we follow Starbuck, the camera behind her as she jogs through the Galactica's corridors—here we get an actual tour of the ship, following a path and learning the space. At certain points the camera shifts characters, so we are with Adama for a time, then back to Starbuck, then to a group of engineers on the flight deck, then into the ship's bridge. By the end of this scene we've visited most of the essential spaces on the ship; we are beginning to learn this virtual world. At other points, however, the camera moves outside the ship, so we are given a look at the ship as a whole, the "god's-eye" perspective. In addition, there are ship schematics on the walls of the bridge, maps that help us understand the totality of this space. The same alternation occurs during the frequent dogfights we witness. At some moments we ride with single pilots in their fighters as they battle waves of cylon ships. But these shots are interwoven into shots from inside the Galactica, where we can track their movement on radar, see the entire battle as it plays out.

A large part of *Battlestar Galactica*'s success, as a show, comes from its understanding of how television works and how science fiction might be thoughtfully co-opted to take advantage of how television works. As science fiction it necessarily moves us into a new space, a landscape entirely different from our own. As a television show, its spaces must grow episode by episode. *Battlestar Galactica* recognized that a particular sort of science fiction plot would take advantage of this particular strength, that fusing the two—science fiction and television—in just the right combination, might redefine what a TV storyworld could do.

POST-APOCALYPTIC WORLDS

Battlestar Galactica is not merely a science fiction series, though. To be more precise it exemplifies a very specific species of science fiction, the post-apocalyptic narrative. The characters and places in the series are unfamiliar to us, but the fact remains that their worlds have been destroyed. We find

Figure 6.1. We follow Starbuck as she jogs through the Galactica corridors. *Battlestar Galactica*, miniseries

ourselves not merely in an "other" space, but along with the characters having lost our space and needing to find another.

Critic Leslie Fiedler sees all science fiction as "post-apocalyptic," arguing it encodes "the myth of the end of man, of the transcendence or transformation of the human—a vision quite different from that of the extinction of our species by the Bomb, which seems stereotype rather than archetype" (1965, 508). His point here is that post-apocalyptic fiction—(all science fiction from his point of view) doesn't simply point to man's annihilation; rather it offers up new opportunities to explore man's behaviors, to imagine what we might perhaps become were our contemporary reality to disappear suddenly. It considers, how might we rebuild in such circumstances.

In fact, a good deal of science fiction, but especially post-apocalyptic science fiction, bears an important relationship to social contract theory and its emphasis on "building" human communities. Social contract theory, in a writer like Hobbes, Locke, or Rousseau, begins by thinking human society back to square one, imagining us in our most primitive state, and then considering how communities and governments might eventually form. Relying on this mental experiment, each social contract philosopher could claim his version of the "ideal" government as the most logical or "natural." Whatever their particular preference—democracy, monarchy, dictatorship—the questions they raised about these scenarios remained pretty much the same: How might humans have acted before society developed, when we were perfectly free to do as we wished? What forces might have led individual, isolated humans to band together into larger groups? How might those forces have dictated relationships between these various groups? What events might have led to the institution of laws and governments?

John Locke's *Two Treatises of Government* (1690), for example—a key text in the development of democracy in America, Britain, and France—includes a chapter titled "the State of Nature," which begins,

> To understand political power aright, and derive it from its original, we must consider what state all men are naturally in and that is a state of perfect freedom to order their actions and dispose of their possessions and persons as they think fit, within the bounds of the law of nature, without asking leave, or depending upon the will of any other man. (1960)

Locke's investigation of "political power," here thinks man back to "his natural state"—individual, alone, pre-society.

Over the course of the nineteenth century, developments in anthropology and sociology, to say nothing of the effect wielded by Darwin's *On the Origin of Species* called these versions of early human societies into serious question. At the same time, the rise of the industrial age and the accompanying rise in our ability to destroy ourselves on a massive scale led, in the twentieth century, to a very different twist on these narratives: the post-apocalyptic novel. Such novels served the same essential purpose as social contract philosophy, but rather than placing mankind in some original "primal" state, they reduced the world to rubble as a means of forcing the characters to start society anew. Two hundred years of history had developed the novel into an almost perfect vehicle for telling such tales, with the particular benefit that a reader could experience along with the characters the challenges of rebuilding society.

Often the post-apocalyptic story involves situations somewhat more complicated than those imagined by social contract theorists. In *The Walking Dead*, for example, the characters aren't simply tasked with rebuilding society; instead, they must try to do so while simultaneously battling zombies at every turn. Even so, these works almost always explore the social and political ramifications of the new situation. The means of getting back to square one may have become more violent, but the same questions that Locke and Rousseau struggled with remain: On what basis do we re-create a social order? What sort of government would work best in such extreme circumstances? Can such a thing as "morality" continue to exist—should it—in the face of absolute chaos and catastrophe, or does human survival trump every other consideration?

John Wyndham's novel *The Day of the Triffids* (1951) is among the first modern examples of this type of narrative. In it, most of the world's population have been blinded by a mysterious green meteor shower and are now being harried by triffids, an intelligent, ambulatory species of carnivorous plant. In the wake of the initial event—the blinding—government institutions break down and new, more primitive political structures grow up in their place. Several warlords, for instance, seize control by kidnapping the few remaining sighted individuals and forcing them to lead work-gangs that scavenge for supplies. Like a good social contract theorist, Wyndham points out the holes in this plan: the sighted easily counter the might-is-right approach by lying to their blind captors and leading them into danger at the first opportunity. In contrast, some remnants of the government propose using the blind as slaves for the sighted; the novel rejects this suggestion as well. In the end, Wyndham seems to advocate a communal system, one in which a small band of survivors—a mix of the sighted and the blind—learn to subsist off the land using their varying skills and abilities. In a final move, however, one that once more hearkens back to social contract theory, this small group eventually realizes it cannot protect itself indefinitely from the triffids and decides to join a larger colony. In such a way, the resurrection of large-scale government begins.

Wyndham recognizes he is building, or rebuilding, a world, a new place that comes with new rules that demand new behaviors. As readers, we are essentially blind in this new world. He addresses this narrative problem, first by having his central character, Bill Masen, begin the story blind as well. Masen wakes alone in a silent hospital, his eyes still bandaged following a recent surgery. In practical terms, his temporary "blindness" explains why once he removes the bandages he can still see—he was not subjected to the blinding green flash. But the device also puts him in the position of "awakening" to this changed world: his eyes (and ours along with his) see things anew, the ideal metaphor given that he awakens to a *new* world (*The Walking Dead* cleverly mimics this plot device, with Rick waking in the pilot episode completely alone in an abandoned hospital, with no idea the world has changed while he lay unconscious). Additionally, Wyndham has Masen move through the landscape, from the streets and back alleys of London to the Sussex countryside, a plotline that develops this world's physical space: we learn to navigate this space right along with him.

As I have tried to stress a number of times already, all narrative presents virtual worlds,[1] but novelistic and filmic worlds are generally limited in terms of plot structure in comparison to what a television series can offer. A dystopian or post-apocalyptic novel or film might contain enough space to explore one or two potential political systems, but ultimately both are limited by the fact that they must come to an end. Plot resolution defines these media, and in many respects it is a strength. *Day of the Triffids* offers us an ideological conclusion—the self-reliance of small human groups that will eventually grow into a new, better version of society. But we aren't told how that community will continue to survive and grow long term. We don't know what will happen when various new factions inevitably clash over values, or when a charismatic leader manages to seize control of the government. We aren't told how they will deal with threats from other, more aggressive communities. Indeed, the novel ends before the small band of characters who have survived so well for so many years actually arrive at the larger commune. For the space of a novel, ending at this point makes perfect structural sense: giving us information about this new colony would require Wyndham essentially begin again. As readers we expect it to end; we want it to end; and we want things neatly resolved. So Wyndham shows us the small-scale version, *and* that it cannot survive on its own but must integrate with other like-minded societies. We *assume* the larger colony will work much the same as the smaller one, and we must be satisfied with this resolution.

In contrast, the television show, because of its relatively greater open-endedness—particularly the fact that, in most cases, we *don't* know when a series will end—offers a more expansive story that can spread out into a more expansive universe.[2] *Its* form demands that "resolutions" must always be *undone*. By necessity, the post-apocalyptic television series does this especially well, pushing deeply into the social and political questions it raises and at the same time pushing against the physical boundaries of its imagined reality. The result is a more complex exploration of social structures than offered in a novel: the contemporary televsion series doesn't offer easy solutions—or in most cases any solutions—to problems.

THE WALKING DEAD

From its first episode, *The Walking Dead* raises important questions about humanity, how might we behave in extreme situations, for instance, and how might various social systems fare under stress? Characters must define in the pilot episode what these "walkers" are and how they should be treated. Initially, for instance, Rick hesitates to kill them, unwilling to accept they are no longer humans. The first human he encounters, Morgan Jones, helps him overcome his fears, but Morgan faces a more extreme version of the same crisis: can he bring himself to kill his own wife now that she has turned? As Rick moves on in search of his family, he re-encounters a walker from before, a girl without legs who pulls herself by her arms through an empty park. Where before he simply avoided the girl, this time Rick shoots her in the head; he has not only come to terms with killing these walkers, he has found a way to justify killing them as an act of mercy.

Yet the show is unwilling to settle for easy answers. In episode 2, "Guts," Rick tells the racist Merle that racism is pointless now. In this new world "race and color no longer matter." The line suggests maybe something good might come from all this misery—we might establish a new, better society; faced with walkers, we might grow closer as human beings. Merle refuses to let go of his prejudices, and in fact they become even more ingrained when the black character T-Dog loses the key to Merle's handcuffs, leaving Merle to saw off his own hand in order to escape from the walkers. The show's producers don't justify racism in this scene, but they do undermine Rick's easy solutions. Merle's racism may be strengthened here by happenstance—it may be based on a single event rather than a larger reality, it may ultimately be illogical—but his anger, if not his broad application of it toward all blacks, *is* justified. The event makes clear that racism and sexism will not magically disappear even when survivors must rely on one another for their very lives. For Merle, walkers don't simply create an "us vs. them" mentality; in fact, they tend to reinforce his already racist belief system.

Over and over again the show sets up one social or political principle, only to undo it. In the beginning, for example, family seems to matter most. Before the apocalypse, Rick and his best friend and colleague Shane sit in their squad car talking about the difference between men and women, and though Rick clearly seems to have trouble relating to his wife, we also sense that his family is what matters to him most. This sense is heightened when he is shot while chasing a fugitive ("Shane, you do not tell Lori that happened! Ever!"), and then again after the apocalypse when his only mission becomes to find his wife and son. The importance of family is further reinforced by his encounter with the character Jones, who fiercely protects his young son and cannot bring himself to kill his zombie wife. Yet before the episode is over, we discover that, post-apocalypse, Rick's wife Laurie has fallen into an affair with Shane, shattering any hope we might have that finding his family will return Rick's life to normal.

Science seems to offer hope, and the group heads to the CDC, but in the space of two episodes ("Wildfire" and "TS-19") we discover that science, too, is a dead end. For a time, after they leave Herschel's farm, Rick sets himself up as "dictator"; this collapses when the group encounter a real dictator in the figure of the Governor. Religion occasionally offers some solace, but never for long: Rick prays for an answer in a backwoods church just before a passing hunter accidently shoots Carl; later we encounter Father Gabriel Stokes who, while clinging to his unwillingness to kill walkers, locked his church and allowed his parishioners to die outside. Pacifism, utilitarianism, agrarianism, anarchy—all appear at one point or another, some many times, but none offers anything like a solution to the situation. Good television can never settle for one-dimensional solutions. Rather television's strength is to constantly complicate situations, to unsettle every attempt to establish normalcy. As a result, the small society at the heart of the show is forced to develop and evolve; we, as the audience, experience this fictional universe's reality to its fullest extent.

This filling out is accomplished in a physical sense as well so that the geography of this world expands over time. For one thing, the characters remain constantly on the move. Just as no social principle can solve their problems, no place can ever provide true safety. For an episode, a half season, or even a whole season, the survivors may find a temporary shelter—the quarry, the CDC, Herschel's farm, the prison compound—but these never last. They become localized spaces to explore for a time, but they are always abandoned in the end. As a result of this constant movement, though, we get to see more of this world: an abandoned city post-apocalypse, a rural farm that has miraculously survived, and a prison left to fend for itself. Because these characters must move, the storyworld space expands and becomes increasingly real for us as viewers.

But we explore not just the exterior landscape in Georgia; interiors matter as well. Every location must be rigorously checked for walkers. Characters search through the CDC, the prison complex, the buildings in Woodbury, grocery stores, pharmacies, churches, schools, hospitals; we experience every nook and cranny of this virtual reality along with them. So too the characters all make their own individual journeys, both physical and metaphorical. During season 2, Shane changes dramatically after raiding the local school to retrieve a respirator. Daryl roams the forest in search of Sophia, injuring himself when he falls down a hillside. In his delirious state, he confronts his brother Merle in his imagination, and faces his guilt over having left Merle behind. During the second half of season 4, the band split into smaller factions. Each remaining episode from the season follows one of these factions through another part of the countryside before all of them eventually converge at a train station known as Terminus.

The signs of movement, the railroad leading to Terminus for example, are everywhere. Dale's RV plays a key role in the first two seasons. It reminds us of a particular kind of travel, long-term, yet not permanent. It bears the battle scars from confrontations with the walkers, yet it also serves as a beacon of hope, the suggestion that perhaps the tragedy that has befallen the world is only temporary, an extended vacation after which everything will return to normal. The group travels the roads, the railroad tracks; they encounter abandoned cars. In the pilot, we see Rick riding into Atlanta on a horse, the shot filmed from well above, his own slow movement into the city contrasted with the bumper to bumper traffic jam of empty cars in the outbound lane beside him. Later, we find another character, Glenn—having used a car alarm as a distraction to save his friends—driving at high speed down this same highway, yelling in triumph. Daryl, the tracker, knows the spaces of the forest. Glenn, we discover, knows the streets of Atlanta because he "delivered pizzas" before the apocalypse. Maps appear over and over again (including one in the opening credits).

And the sense of space we gain from movement is intensified by god's-eye camera work as well. The shot of Rick riding into Atlanta—the view of this world from above—is echoed throughout the series. When Rick is caught beneath a tank at the end of the first episode, the camera pulls straight up to show the tank surrounded by walkers and continues up to show walkers pouring from every side street. We realize just how trapped Rick is (a claustrophobia that defines the series), but the shot additionally situates Rick within the space of Atlanta. Many other scenes in Atlanta occur atop buildings, offering panoramic views of the ruined cityscape.

This alternating camerawork continues. Episode 2 opens on Dale, standing guard atop his RV, but the camera moves down to ground level, where we follow first Amy and then Lori, on a tour through their makeshift camp. We're left with a more complete view of their shelter and the surrounding area from having tracked them.

In a 2012 interview, showrunner Glen Mazzara insisted that the *Walking Dead* survivors would never find a safe haven:

> There is no safe haven in this world. I want to make that clear. At the end of our season two finale that farm is overtaken and that farm was that last safe haven,

Figure 6.2. Dale keeps watch for walkers atop his RV.
***The Walking Dead*, 1.2**

and there's no safe haven in that world. I want to be very clear about that. No one is safe. There is no safe haven. (2012, n.p.)

Later in the interview he adds that the show is unlikely to offer any resolution when it eventually reaches its finale: "It's not about necessarily having an answer that sums it all up with a pretty bow. This show is more about how these people survive in this apocalypse." This explains why the show has been so successful and so influential on the development of television generally—it recognizes that its virtual world must continue to grow, both in terms of pushing its spatial boundaries and in terms of questioning how society can survive within these spaces.

A STALLED *REVOLUTION*

The fact that television has discovered this unique ability to offer ever-expanding landscapes though, doesn't necessarily mean it always uses this ability effectively. NBC's post-apocalyptic series *Revolution* (2012–2014) provides a useful example of how an evolving television world can suddenly stagnate. While *Revolution* began with a clear direction, by the second season it faltered, in large part because it stopped exploring the possibilities of the world it had initially imagined.

In the beginning *Revolution* constructed a vibrant alternative reality, and it worked hard to give us opportunities to experience that reality fully. As the lights first begin to go out, during the pilot's opening scenes, the camera tracks out of the Matheson's home moving upward (reminding us of Rick trapped beneath the tank), so we see the roof of their house; as the scope widens we watch first the neighborhood, then the city, the country, and finally the entire globe go dark. For a moment, the show's world lies spread out in its entirety beneath us. We recognize it as our world in a sense, but as we watch, it transforms into something new: a virtual, fictional version of the world we know: a world without power. In the next scenes, dated as "fifteen years later," we're given a quick tour of famous cities and landmarks—the St. Louis arch, the Golden Gate Bridge, the Capitol in D.C. The overgrown wilderness that surrounds these landmarks together with their decrepit conditions emphasizes both how much time has passed and how much civilization has declined during that period. At the same time, though, this montage provides a sense of this new America, reorienting us to the altered space we will inhabit over the course of the series.

As in *The Walking Dead*, the camera highlights the space of this universe from above, but the producers also use character movement within that space to help us understand it on a concrete level. This too is established at the beginning of the blackout: as Ben and Rachel Matheson and their children watch the lights go out at home, Ben's brother Miles and his friend Monroe experience the event from Miles's car, now stranded along with hundreds of others on an interstate highway. As each car's headlights wink out, one by one, we're reminded that the blackout will limit movement in this new world. Without this movement, society will fragment into isolated communities; it will have to begin again. At the same time, movement becomes, from this instant, an important goal; survival in this new environment will require knowing it well and only moving through it can achieve that. As they prepare to leave their home for the last time, Ben and Rachel tell the young Charlie, "We are gonna do a lot of walking. It's like Dora [the explorer]: we are gonna walk right out of the city."

Fifteen years later, we find a grown up Charlie and her younger brother Danny exploring the woods near their small community. It turns out the forest growth covers over a long disused highway where the teenagers discover an RV left rusting on its side. As in *The Walking Dead*, the vehicle operates as a powerful early symbol of movement. Though long discarded, it suggests possibilities, opportunities for exploration, and even at this early point, before the real action has even begun, we understand that Charlie yearns to travel.

Inside the RV she finds a postcard from Chicago—a picture of Wrigley Field—and we learn that she collects postcards, keeping them in an old lunchbox hidden at an abandoned fairground. They connect her to the past, but they also connect her to the larger world beyond her small community.

Figure 6.3. Charlie and Danny discover an abandoned RV.
***Revolution*, 1.1**

Sitting alone, flipping through these pictures, she shows us—again—the space of this larger world. Or rather, she shows us the space that once *was*, an undamaged twin of her own. But we already know the space defined by the *series'* present is quite different. That was established in the opening montage of landmarks. We see it again, though, when Charlie arrives in Chicago looking for her uncle Miles. The first sight she confronts in the city is Wrigley Field, the "real" embodiment—in her universe—of the faded picture: a stadium now crumbling and overgrown with ivy. For us, as viewers, the scene offers a notable transition from one reality to another, and the postcard suits this transition especially well. It features an image drawn from our own media-centric universe, an image we accept as "genuine"—a picture postcard. This is how Chicago appears to us. Like Charlie, we know our world through pictures—pictures on postcards, pictures in magazines, pictures on the internet, pictures on television. The trick the postcard achieves is to move us from an image we know and accept in our own world—a "real" picture of Wrigley Field—into the world of the show we are watching, which—it turns out—is just another sort of picture. Just as that image of the baseball park changes for Charlie, then, it changes for us as well, both within the context of the show and in the broader context of watching the show.

Charlie's movement through this post-apocalyptic virtual reality doesn't end with her arrival in Chicago. She and her compatriots spend several episodes pursuing her brother Danny, who has been taken by the Monroe Militia; they spend several more episodes fleeing from the Militia after having rescued Danny; and finally, they race the Militia to a former Defense Department base in Colorado from where they hope the power can be restored. The group travel by horse, wagon, boat, steam train, moving through Chicago; Grant Park, Illinois; Lowell, Indiana; Philadelphia; Atlanta; Lagrange, Missouri; and Colorado. Along the way, they encounter a wide variety of landscapes, from internment camps, to abandoned amusement parks and train stations. Each move stretches our knowledge of the series' physical space, so that the virtual world widens with every episode.

At the same time, as a contemporary version of social contract theory, *Revolution* considers a number of possible social and political solutions to the post-apocalyptic chaos, thinking in turn about the various advantages and disadvantages each offers. Reduced to a state of "nature," those who remain after the blackout must deal with life after "civilization," facing basic human needs like hunger but struggling at the same time to hold on to some measure of "humanity." In episode 2, for instance, we're presented with a scene from the past, from early in the blackout in which a looter holds a gun to young Charlie's head and demands the Matheson's food stores. Already in the immediate aftermath of the blackout society is breaking down. The

Mathesons quickly learn lessons about the dangers around them, and they themselves become hardened by these dangers.

As Charlie's journey unfolds over the first season, we encounter a number of different social models that have sprung up over the fifteen years since the lights went out. The Monroe Militia, of course, represents the largest and most threatening of these, a government that, while it has managed to restore law and order has done so by imposing permanent martial law. In flashbacks, we see that the impulse to form this particular government sprang from the best of intentions, a pact between Miles and Monroe to root out reckless outlaws and protect the weak. Yet it has devolved into the worst sort of dictatorship in which Monroe will stop at nothing to achieve his own personal ends, destroying anyone who stands in his way. Among the other lessons here, the Monroe Militia demonstrates that no government, no matter how well-intentioned, can ever truly rise above corruption without some sort of checks on absolute power.

But over the course of the first season we're shown other models as well, small pockets of civilization surviving as best they can. Ben Matheson and his two children, for example, live in a small communal space, carved out of a suburban cul-de-sac, in which the members look out for one another and share the workload. While this works well in the context of the commune itself, we discover in the pilot that the commune's relatively small size—the quality that helps it maintain its stability—also leaves it prey to larger outside forces, in this case the Militia. In "The Plague Dogs" (episode 4), Charlie's group encounters a man who has abandoned society altogether, replacing human companions with dogs; in "Sex and Drugs" (episode 6), they must deal with Drexel, a warlord who has created a fiefdom out of his stash of lifesaving drugs; in "The Children's Crusade" (episode 7), they discover a group of children whose parents were killed by the Militia and who have now formed their own society. The cities they enter are mostly run like the Wild West, and there are bands of "rebel" fighters committed to restoring the now heavily mythologized U.S. government to power.

Often the show seems to advocate family relationships as the best answer to re-establishing a new social order. We are frequently reminded that family matters more than anything else. Charlie, after all, begins her adventure in pursuit of her brother, and after locating her uncle Miles demands he help her: "You're gonna help me get him back [. . .] because we're family." In the face-off that occurs midseason between Miles and Monroe, we learn that Monroe considers Miles a brother. Yet Miles is not, in fact, his brother, and at least at this early moment in the series, that signifies an important difference. Miles chooses his family without hesitation: brother-*like* relationships will not do. This emphasis on family might have threatened the show, since it put ideology up against the problem of television's open-endedness. A series such as this cannot rest in a single solution. In the end, the show survived because it complicated its answer (Danny dies; Charlie finds herself at odds with her mother, Rachel; Miles turns out to have had an affair with Rachel) and as a result, didn't stop exploring.

The close connection between movement and the exploration of social systems takes a particularly interesting turn at the season's end, when, as the power is at last restored one member of the group, calling himself a "patriot," launches several nuclear missiles at American cities. As we watch, the missiles spread across a map on a computer screen, a technological stand-in for the Earth we saw from a distance when the blackout occurred. The moment tears down two more potential political structures—first the "patriots" who hope to restore the U.S. government; but also the "technologists" who believe restoring electricity to the world will somehow return society to a state of law and order. The patriot commits suicide, leaving his ideology to serve as the second season's chief antagonist. The technologists realize immediately they have made a mistake and shut off the power for good. The final episode then not only resolves the first season's plotline—the search for a means of restoring the power—but through that digital map reminds us of the space we have traversed, both literally and figuratively, over the course of the season.

From an economic standpoint, the show did well in its first season, averaging 9.8 million viewers per episode and earning a full second season commitment from NBC. During this second season, however, it could never seem to recapture the emphasis on space and movement it had previously established. For virtually the entire season, Miles and Rachel remain headquartered in the town of Willoughby, Texas, fending off various representatives of the Patriots. The episodes during this second season are typically divided into three storylines. Charlie's pursuit of vengeance against Monroe, does involve movement. The other two storylines, however, remain essentially static, and in the end the show itself seems to stop exploring possibilities. As one reviewer Tim Surette put it, "a whole season dedicated to stopping the Patriots got boring by episode 6" (2014, n.p.). Surette goes on to point out that the science of the show got lost as well, which is another way of saying that we stopped learning the "rules" of this new world; the world stopped growing. With nothing really left to explore, spatially, socially, or scientifically, *Revolution* simply folded in on itself.

JERICHO

As I suggested in chapter 3, movement in space doesn't always have to be external. As Jason Mittell points out, a show can thrive off of internal movement as well. In either case, the important element is the movement itself. *Jericho,* while it was cancelled after just a season and a half, manages to do what *Revolution* couldn't—continue to push its boundaries. However, it serves as a good example of how this can be done internally rather than externally.

Jericho was equally short-lived—lasting just a season and a half—but it garnered positive reviews and developed a cult-following. Online forums still talk wistfully about the possibility the show might be revived in some form. In many ways the whole series was set up much like the second season of *Revolution*. That is, the action occurs almost entirely within the city limits of a single town; only occasionally do characters make forays into other locations. *Jericho*, however, found a way to grow its world by filtering the outside world through this single town. In the end this unique approach serves as another important metaphor for TV worlds in general.

As in both *Revolution* and *The Walking Dead*, *Jericho* emphasizes movement, but even more than these shows, after the apocalyptic event it cuts off that movement absolutely. Free travel in and outside of *Jericho* is part of the world that *was*—our first image of Jake is from the window of a train, and we next find him driving the stereotypical American muscle car along a heartland highway. Later, when his return to town turns emotionally difficult, he takes to his car again as an escape: "Gotta get back to San Diego." During the first episode, however, when the world suddenly changes, this movement stops. When the first mushroom cloud appears over the horizon, we see it reflected in the windows of a school bus (a stand-in for the RVs of *Walking Dead* and *Revolution*), an image that juxtaposes transportation with the apocalypse. As school teacher Heather Lisinski watches the cloud rise, the bus hits a fleeing deer, stranding the children in the middle of nowhere. At roughly the same moment, Jake runs headlong into another car, ending his "escape." Meanwhile Emily, who hasn't yet realized what has happened, runs into a flock of blackbirds, who fall dead en masse, blocking the road to Denver. The show's point has to do with the inability to escape into the outside world—the "event" will force those in the town to remain where they are and learn to deal with one another. Rather than travel through a variety of social systems, the producers instead force the town itself to grow and evolve as a society.

Immediately after the explosion, for example, the townspeople must confront their own fears, fears that put the stability of the town in jeopardy. Gracie Leigh, who owns the town market, responds to the crisis by raising her prices; at the same time, the people in the town begin to panic, fearing the loss of the food supply, and looting breaks out. In another early episode a large portion of the town's population must hide in the local mine to avoid radiation poisoning. While there, Scott Rennie experiences claustrophobia and begins to hyperventilate. Another character, Gray, makes the decision to remove him

Figure 6.4. Heather Lisinski watches a mushroom cloud from her school bus. ***Jericho*, 1.1**

from the rest of the crowd, and we learn later that Rennie was allowed to die of a stress-induced heart attack rather than upset the rest of the crowd. Mimi Clark an IRS agent who has come to collect back taxes from the Richmond farm continues to hold on to her belief in the U.S. government, even in the face of clear evidence that government has fallen. Eric finds himself caught between an affair he began before the bombs fell and staying true to his wife now that circumstances have changed. Each situation raises questions about how human beings would or should behave in the wake of disaster, how we might handle a "reboot."

Increasingly, though, as the series develops, the world outside Jericho becomes the enemy. Robert Hawkins warns a fireman in the pilot episode, "You might not want the wrong people knowing Jericho is still here," and his words turn out to be prophetic. In fact, the town is immediately threatened from the outside in episode 2 ("Fallout") in the form of a coming storm that may bring radiation fallout with it. The episode establishes that, while the town may remain the center of the action, they always have an eye—in a quite literal sense—on the horizon. As the action of securing shelter for the townspeople unfolds in this episode, we continually return to images of the storm as it approaches, a reminder of the larger world outside Jericho.

Sometimes the fear of the outside comes up against the town's ethics, as when they learn a band of refugees with radiation poisoning has made it to a point just outside of town. The town is split between those who feel they must help these survivors and those who feel that to do so would put the town itself in danger. In other cases, the outside world presents examples of failed social experiments. In "9:02" (episode 6) the town is subjected to its own bomb, this one an EMP explosion that cripples their electrical devices. Later, in the same episode, thieves from outside manage to steal the town's food. In episode 8 ("Rogue River"), Jake visits the nearby town of Rogue River looking for medicine to help his father. There he discovers that a former military contractor, Ravenwood, has taken over and imposed martial law. Eventually, Jericho must make a stand against a Ravenwood invasion. In the second half of this first season, a new threat arises—the nearby town of New Bern—and Jericho must again stand together to turn away this threat to their survival. When an actual military force arrives from Cheyenne at the beginning of season 2, we learn little by little it is rife with corruption and in league with members of Ravenwood.

Meanwhile, other plot developments help us better understand the physical space outside the city. Initially, the townspeople aren't sure what has happened; they hope that perhaps only Denver was destroyed. However, they piece together a more complete story. Dale's parents call from Atlanta and leave a phone message just as a bomb explodes, confirmation that the explosions occurred nationwide. Every episode after brings the town a new piece of information that helps to flesh out the world outside. They catch snatches of television that suggest who the enemy might be. They begin to learn which cities were hit by nuclear strikes (and early on we see a complete map of these on Robert Hawkins's computer). Refugees arrive with information about towns placed under martial law. Residents of Jericho travel to a nearby town where they find a bulletin board full of travelers' stories that help to fill in some of the blanks. Slowly Jericho learns that other pockets of civilization remain, and eventually that several versions of the federal government have been established in places unaffected by the bombs.

In this case, the series expands its virtual space by mirroring what we, as an audience, experience when watching a television series. These characters must try to piece together a world outside their own, using only little bits of information; we do the same along with them—learning the geography and the rules of this "new" world, filling in the various aspects of its existence as they do. In this way, the show offers a kind of model for how television works: in one sense the viewer remains stationary before the screen; in another sense, she explores a vast virtual reality within that screen. The show itself pieces that reality together one scene at a time.

If children's television marks one entry point into TV worlds, the post-apocalyptic drama offers another. In fact, television's coming-of-age over the past two decades has not coincidentally occurred at the same time the post-apocalyptic drama has become a schedule mainstay. A whole host of such shows have premiered since 2000, including *Helix*, *Defiance*, *12*

Monkeys, *Falling Skies*, *The Last Ship*, *Outcasts*, and *The 100*. *The Walking Dead* garnered some of the highest ratings in cable history, and has spawned a spinoff, *Fear the Walking Dead*. While the genre's initial rise might be attributed to post-9/11 angst,[3] much of its continuing popularity has to do with the nature of television itself and its newly discovered power to explore its own fictional landscapes. By definition, the post-apocalyptic narrative involves doing away with the world as it exists, wiping the slate clean as it were. This makes world-building a necessity in such works. As a result, these TV series offer the perfect venue for television to explore its strengths. And because these shows *must* "call worlds into being" for their viewers, they offer useful illustrations for thinking about how *all* television series do so.

NOTES

1. In fact, in "Epic and Novel," literary theorist Mikhail Bakhtin writes that the novel involves "the incomplete process of a world-in-the-making, and is stamped with the seal of inconclusiveness"; "For the first time in artistic-ideological consciousness, time and the world become historical: they unfold albeit at first still unclearly and confusedly, as becoming, as an uninterrupted movement into a real future, as a unified, all-embracing and unconcluded process" (55). This argument resonates with my own arguments about the nature of television as an open-ended artistic genre. Bakhtin actually prefigures my work here, arguing that the novel is only one step along a lengthy path in the development of narrative: "In many respects the novel has anticipated, and continues to anticipate, the future development of literature as a whole" (35). I would apply the same sentiment to television as a genre: it represents an important development in narrative, but one that anticipates *future* developments. Mikhail Bakhtin, "Epic and Novel," *The Dialogic Imagination* (Austin: University of Texas Press, 1981).

2. I should note here that this quality is also true of much graphic fiction—*The Walking Dead* comic book series, for example. In fact, I would argue that, while it can't quite compete with the visual sophistication of television, one explanation for the relatively recent rise in graphic fiction's mainstream popularity is its skillful use of open-ended seriality.

3. John Walliss and James Aston note, "there has [. . .] been a significant increase in apocalyptic imagery and themes post-9/11 across a variety of popular media" (2011, 54). Mathias Nilges argues more specifically that the ugliness of the post-9/11 world pushed narrative toward images of "beautiful destruction," a kind of purification of the complexities we inhabit day-to-day: writing about *The Day After Tomorrow* and *I am Legend*, Nilges explains, "What is more striking than the terrible beauty of the disaster itself, however, is the beautiful representation of life after the destruction" (2010, 24).

Chapter 7

"Walk the Straight and Narrow Track"

Developing Worlds

If *Battlestar Galactica* and *The Walking Dead* show how science fiction can be employed to powerful effect on television, how it can be made to take advantage of television's natural strengths as a medium, *The Wire* demonstrates how the police drama genre can be adapted to do the same. In this chapter I examine *The Wire* and to a lesser extent two police dramas that followed closely in its footsteps—*Justified* and *Fargo*. In the same way *Battlestar* and *The Walking Dead* transform the traditional science fiction series into intricately developed storyworlds, these series transform the police drama, fusing the spatial elements inherent in the genre itself with television's capacity to generate expansive virtual realities. Where science fiction offers a useful illustration of how a TV narrative establishes its world, these series illustrate some of the means by which TV worlds can be developed.

THE WIRE

The Wire has been hailed as among the best series in television history. In a 2013 list of the greatest TV shows ever, *Entertainment Weekly* ranked it number one; *Rolling Stone*, listed it second, behind only *The Sopranos*. Literary theorist Walter Benn Michaels, described it as "the most serious and ambitious fictional narrative of the twenty-first century so far" (qtd. in Vint 2013, introduction). The show is remarkable for a number of reasons, as Sherryl Vint points out in her insightful book on the series, *The Wire*. As social commentary, it was "distinguished by the complexity of its narrative and its refusal to restrict its focus to individual crimes isolated from the social context in which criminality is produced" (2013, introduction). As a work of art, it "pushes television in new directions" (introduction). As important as the complexity of its narrative and themes, however, is the way in which it develops its space.

The Wire is set in Baltimore, and in its first episodes it sets up like a traditional police drama. The police in this particular instance, are investigating the drug trade on the west side of the city. The drug kingpin, Avon Barksdale, and his second in command, Stringer Bell, have committed a string of murders over the past eighteen months, culminating in the death of a state's witness in a trial against Barksdale's nephew, D'Angelo. Central character, detective James McNulty is determined to catch Barksdale and put a stop to both the murders and the drug trade itself. Typical of many police series, his zealous efforts are stymied at every turn by his superiors who view his crusade as a waste of resources when making quick arrests of several lower level dealers would make for a more impressive news story. Despite these obstacles, McNulty manages to piece together a special unit—though it is made up of several rejects from other departments—to investigate Barksdale's activities. The first season then plays out as the expected game of cat and mouse.

The goal in a traditional police drama—from *Columbo* to *NYPD Blue* to *Law and Order* is to "uncover,"—to determine who committed a given crime and to understand how it occurred. In the final season of *Major Crimes*, for example, serial killer Phillip Stroh, a recurring character throughout the series, returns to menace Los Angeles. His first act is to kill a district attorney, and the police scramble to figure out how he managed to pull off the crime. But the plot thickens when it becomes clear that Stroh has a more elaborate plan in mind. Frustrating their efforts, he seems always to be one step ahead of the police. In order to catch him, they must first discover how he manages to elude them, then work out his master plan, and finally capture him before he can kill again.

Spaces matter throughout a show like this. Most obviously, the police need to uncover the space where Stroh actually is. They must search through spaces, learn spaces, make guesses about his movements, and themselves move in response. In this particular case, spaces are linked in another way—through surveillance equipment. The reason Stroh has been able to stay ahead of the police is because he has hired a technical expert to infiltrate their space—the squad room—and install monitoring equipment. As we watch the detectives sort through clues in the case, so does Stroh. He knows what is happening in their space, knows the spaces they plan to explore, and as a result is able to map out his own movements so as to avoid detection. For their part, the police must piece together these clues to reconstruct what occurred. That is, they must re-create in a virtual sense the crime scene, must work out what took place in that space, must be able to imagine it, much like any reader with any storyworld.

Part of what *The Wire* does is amplify these elements of a crime drama. In one episode during season 1, McNulty and his partner Bunk Moreland investigate a murder that might connect to Barksdale and Stringer. The landlord lets them into the apartment where the murder took place and they begin walking through the crime scene, piecing events together as they go. They scatter crime scene photos around the kitchen floor, overlaying their reality with the reality that existed on the night of the crime. They pull out police reports listing the height of the victim and use measuring tape to determine where the killer might have stood and where the bullets might have wound up. As a result, they manage to discover a bullet lodged in the refrigerator door, missed by the original investigators. They only find this bullet though because they have inhabited the space, re-creating the crime in the place where it occurred. The entire scene takes less than five minutes, but it illustrates in a condensed form precisely how space matters in a crime drama.

But space matters in larger ways to this series. The police target, Avon Barksdale is a mysterious figure who has managed to keep a low profile for a number of years. The police know where the major crimes are occurring—in a low-rent apartment complex known as the "towers," and another nearby set of "low rise" apartments. However, they have no idea where Barksdale himself operates. He has no known place of residence, for instance, and no one can even find a picture of him. In fact McNulty and his team spend much of the first season just trying to get a glimpse of him: "This case"—McNulty complains at one point, "We're never where we need to be."

In their quest to nab Barksdale, the police work to infiltrate the spaces he controls, to become a part of those spaces. To this end they send in an undercover operative, who "tours" this space and reports back. They recruit a confidential informant—Bubbles—who gives them additional information on what's happening in these spaces. And they set up an elaborate surveillance operation—"the wire"—which allows them to track criminal movements through this space. This system involves two parts. First, the wire itself allows them to tap payphones in the area, to monitor conversations and find out just who is doing what. But in order for this system to work, detectives must also be stationed "in" the area so they can see exactly who is making the call. Most often, this monitoring takes place on nearby rooftops. In the first season, Kima Greggs and her team of narcotics agents spend hours sitting atop neighborhood buildings, using binoculars and cameras to keep track of what is happening below. As we've seen in other series, the result is a "god's-eye view" that contrasts with the movement of the drug dealers and junkies below to give us a complete overview of this space. This plot device turns police work into a useful means of developing the television space. That is, the very process the police go through to understand the space the drug dealers inhabit is the same process we as viewers go through to understand the space of the series. They become stand-ins of a sort for the audience.

Space is also a sign of power in the series, the currency over which power-struggles take place. One kind of power struggle occurs between the police and the drug dealers. That is, Barksdale and his crew work to keep their empire both operational and a secret. He must play a complicated game with his spaces, both maintaining control over them and keeping his distance so he won't be associated with them. The police, meanwhile, seek to gain control of the same spaces, to unseat Barksdale and restore a different kind of order to the streets. This battle plays out a number of times over the first season, as when the detectives do finally catch their first glimpse of Barksdale and try to set up an impromptu tail to find out where he lives. As Lieutenant Daniels barks orders, the police follow the drug dealer from street to street—down one "path" and another—attempting to map out his moves before he makes them and put themselves in the right strategic positions.

But Barksdale is also involved in power struggles with other drug dealers, always needing to reassert control over his territory. Barksdale, we learn, controls the "West" tower drug trade, while another boss, Prop Joe, controls the East. In a late season 1 episode, the two sides meet for a rival game of basketball, a metaphor for the actual, more dangerous power struggle, in which the winner gets bragging rights—as well as a good deal of money—from the loser. A more important metaphor for territory introduced during this first season is the chess board. D'Angelo, who has been given control of the low rises, which he runs from "the pit," finds his teenage lieutenants using a chessboard to play checkers and determines to teach them the real game.

Figure 7.1. Kima keeps an eye on the drug trade from the roof of a nearby building. *The Wire*, 1.2

His description relies on analogies to Barksdale and the boys themselves. Barksdale is "the King," D'Angelo points out. He doesn't often move, but the rest of the pieces have his back so, "He really ain't gotta do shit." The "pawns" on the other hand, those who fight for the king, "they be out the game early." The entire game is about who controls the board's spaces and how long the king can remain hidden and protected.

Season 1 reaches a climax in episodes 10 and 11, "The Cost," and "The Hunt." These episodes bring into focus not only the events of the show but just how tied into these events the particular spaces are, how much the spaces, in fact, dictate the events. The central question throughout the season is never really who the bad guys are but rather *where* they are. In "The Cost," Kima goes undercover in a sting operation to catch some of Barksdale's hired guns. As with everything in the series, her movements in space matter. She is being monitored closely by the rest of her unit. The sting goes bad, however, when Kima is "lost." In their attempt to confuse the police, neighborhood criminals have turned the street signs around so that they face the wrong way, confusing the space. Kima loses track of where she is, and as a result her handlers lose track of her as well. In the few minutes it takes them to relocate her, she is shot.

Throughout episode 11, the police work to sort out what happened, how she got lost, who shot her, and where the perpetrators have gone. All of this again revolves around issues of space. From the scene of the crime, one group of detectives traces the literal footsteps of the shooters, tracking them

Figure 7.2. Major Rawls checks the street signs after Kima has been shot. *The Wire*, 1.10

down back alleys, railroad tracks, complex paths, picking up clues as they go. Meanwhile, another set of detectives convenes at headquarters to examine a map of the area.

There are important thematic points to be made about these spaces. As Lint points out, the struggle between the police and the drug trade is not as simple as it is in most police dramas. Instead, as we discover during this first season, no one's hands are truly clean. Bunk is willing to bend the rules to catch criminals, asking Kima to pick a specific perpetrator out of a lineup even though she never saw him; Ellis and Herc, two grunts on the police detail alternate their time between trying to act tough and trying to pocket drug money from evidence; McNulty himself puts his own children in harm's way by having them tail Stringer Bell through a market. But the show isn't just about demonstrating that police and thieves can often be roughly equivalent in their behaviors both on and off the job. It makes a larger point of showing how the social structures in the city of Baltimore push the various characters into these behaviors. So, for instance, images of the run-down towers are frequently juxtaposed with impressive government buildings downtown, or a scene in which Stringer Bell looks down from a terrace window onto the drug trade going on below him is followed by a scene in which Major Rawls looks out his office window onto the "legal" commerce taking place below him. These moments remind us that these characters inhabit very different spaces. In many ways they exercise their control over these spaces using similar methods, but the difference in the spaces themselves determines on which side of the law they wind up.

Important as well is the fact that these spaces don't change in any significant way by the season's end. While the police have mobilized some drug busts and arrests—have caught Barksdale himself—they have failed to solve the systemic problems that lie behind the drug trade, failed to understand and thus transform the space. Throughout the season the most iconic of these spaces is "the pit," a grass courtyard in the middle of the low rises where D'Angelo oversees drug sales, mostly to street people, while sitting on the back of a ratty orange couch. The producers want us to know this area from every vantage point. We see it from a variety of angles—from above, in panning 360 degree shots, from the couch itself, from the perspective of McNulty and Bunk when they come to question D'Angelo. In the final moments of the final episode, the camera returns to the pit, again circling around it, fixing it as a space. The couch is now black, but otherwise the space is just as it was. The message is clear: the drug trade continues at both the towers and the low rises, unabated. No one has "won" this war.

Instead, the real focus of the first season is that couch and the pit in which it sits; and the dingy basement office the police detail has been forced to occupy all season; and the police station downtown, with its shiny exterior and its several orderly cubicles; and the strip club where Barksdale and Stringer run their empire; and the towers. In another emotional scene from this season, one of D'Angelo's boys, the likeable young man, Wallace, is killed by his friends, Bodie and Poot. At the beginning of the episode we follow him room to room, on a tour through the small apartment he shares with his younger siblings, all of whom he takes care of single-handedly. In the scene in which he is shot, this tour is repeated, though this time the apartment is empty, his siblings having been removed from the line of fire by Poot and Bodie. The first season is meant to explore these spaces and the particular activities that occur there. By its end, we understand these spaces and what happens there, socially, culturally, economically. And while we may judge actions in spots, feel utterly defeated when Wallace is killed for example, in the end our judgments are complicated by the misdeeds that occur on both sides. *The Wire* makes it difficult, if not impossible, to choose a side. Instead, we simply come to know these spaces.

As innovative as season 1 was, season 2 rewrote the rules yet again. We expect this second season to return to the drug trade, to revisit the landscape we learned in season 1. Instead, while the drug trade remains relevant, its spaces fade into the background during this season and we explore an entirely new space, this one the docks near the harbor. In fact, in season 3, producers went so far as destroying the original spaces—the towers and the pit—a sign of the series' need and its intention to expand the space of the series.

Many of the same themes get worked out in this second season. The docks are a maze with their endless stacks of cargo containers. When one container—containing dead women who have been smuggled into the country—is uncovered, the police shift their attention to this new space and to trying to understand that space in order to catch those responsible. Meanwhile, a fierce struggle goes on over control of this space, between the workers, represented by union boss, Frank Sobotka; the shadowy figure of The Greek, who uses the docks as a means to run illegal trade in drugs, guns, counterfeit merchandise, and women; and the wealthy land developers who have plans to do away with the docks altogether and replace them with fancy new apartments. Meanwhile the police set up another "wire" system that allows them to track cargo containers coming into and going out of the docks. This gives them and us a better understanding of how the space works, what kinds of movements are taking place within it.

Season 3, yet again, reinvents the series by shifting the central spaces, but also how those spaces are presented. This season focuses on the police themselves, an admission that they aren't in the end, all that different in their organization from the drug dealers or the corrupt union. They too deserve to have the camera pointed at them. We have already been primed for this realization in seasons 1 and 2. It matters, for instance, that in the first season

McNulty and the rest of his ad hoc squad are forced to run their operation out of a dingy basement space, similar in many ways to the dingy Orlando's where Avon and Stringer oversee their operation. But this point about their similarity is made more obvious in season 3, where the central spaces that matter are those of the police themselves. Specifically, we look at how the various districts are laid out, who controls them, and how they exercise that control.

The key character this season is Major William "Bunny" Colvin, in charge of Baltimore's western district, who, in an effort to reduce crime numbers, makes the bold decision to allow free drug trade in one small area of the district. He dubs this isolated neighborhood Amsterdam, though the drug dealers quickly change it to "Hamsterdam." The area becomes a kind of social experiment, in much the same way the spaces in *The Walking Dead* allow us to see a variety of governing strategies. Over the course of the season, Bunny monitors what happens and is often surprised by the way this "society" behaves when removed from the larger space of the city.

Like the drug dealers from season 1, though, Bunny must simultaneously keep this space operational and keep it secret from his superiors. When, by season's end, it is discovered, he is ultimately fired from the police.

Season 4 is less about new spaces—though the school system does become a new territory to explore—than about perspectives on that space. The central characters in this season are children who are growing up in the area of the drug trade and in many cases working its dangerous "corners." Here we see how and why some of these boys are drawn into that trade while others somehow manage to escape.

Finally, the fifth season of the series focuses on the newspaper industry. Again, this in itself offers a new space to explore, but so, too, it offers us a new perspective on the city at large, that of the reporter—a figure who combines the elements of the "tour" and the "god's-eye" viewpoint. He travels the space, looking for stories, but he also sees it from the newsroom floor, where all of the various stories are fit together by the *Sun*'s editors.

The season was a disappointment to many fans because of how it unfolded. The police narrative returns to the drug trade, as McNulty sets his sights on the man who has replaced Avon Barksdale, Marlo Stanfield. But in his zeal to capture Stanfield, and facing budget limitations caused by another city space—the school system—he decides to invent a serial killer. With media attention focused on these sensational crimes, money is suddenly available again, and McNulty funnels it into one last wire investigation. Many fans were dismayed at McNulty's willingness to invent a crime, but this frustration was magnified by the fact that McNulty's lie is perpetuated by a young reporter, Scott Templeton, who has determined that the best way to get ahead in his business is to invent emotional stories. Simultaneous to McNulty's lie,

Templeton begins to spread the same lie, going so far as to invent a call from the serial killer and running the story as front-page news.

Of course, *The Wire*'s emphasis on space doesn't just show up in terms of its major themes, but permeates the series, through countless smaller moments, symbols and motifs scattered through each episode. In the series' opening scene, for example, we find McNulty sitting on a derelict stoop, where a murder has just occurred, talking philosophically to one of the victim's friends. It doesn't make sense, the friend claims, to have killed "Snot," since he had been doing the same thing for years, "Every Friday night in the alley behind the Cut-Rate." In another episode, Omar Little, a wild-card in the drug trade, draws out a map of the neighborhood in the dirt just before he and his men attack Barksdale's people. Bunk and McNulty have a habit of getting drunk near the railroad tracks. During many of the series' chase scenes helicopters are employed and we're given shots of the streets from above mixed with shots of those same streets from the men on the ground.

THE WIRE'S LEGACY

The Wire set a standard for what a police drama could be—for how it could incorporate television's gift for presenting spaces, and, using the elements of a police drama increase our investment in those spaces. Premiering just two years after *The Wire*'s final episode was another series in which spaces matter—*Justified*. The latter show borrows a great deal from the former. Both, for example, involve central characters, lawmen who are too driven by their jobs, who make far better lawmen than they do human beings. And both develop their spaces in remarkably similar ways.

In the case of *Justified*, the location is Harlan County, Kentucky. And initially, in the first season, the focus is squarely on Marshal Raylan Givens's efforts to put a stop to the drug trade and its related crimes. His major target is the Crowder family, and especially Boyd Crowder and his sister-in-law Ava. As he pursues them, uncovering their organization, we learn the landscape, the major landmarks that define the space, and how they fit together. As with *The Wire*, though, each of the following seasons offers a new plotline though always remaining somewhat tied to the drug narrative. Season 2, for example, shifts to the Bennet Clan and matriarch Mags Bennet who run a family marijuana business; season 3 examines an African American community known as Noble's Holler and run by loan shark Ellstin Limehouse; season 4 relocates to a tent revival on the outskirts of town, led by Billy St. Cyr; season 5 revolves around a Florida crime family, the Crowes, who decide to move into Harlan.

As with *The Wire*, we're introduced to other spaces as well—Ava spends all of the fifth season, for example, in jail, and the series develops this space in detail. And more than *The Wire*, *Justified* expands the boundaries of its space. While there is a good deal of talk in the later seasons of *The Wire* about the Maryland governor's office, the series has enough to do digging into Baltimore's neighborhoods. *Justified*, in contrast, introduces outside forces who connect us to a world outside Harlan County, expanding the virtual landscape. Wynn Duffy, a local representative of the Frankfort, Kentucky, mob who funnel drugs to Harlan, shows up in season 3. Significantly, Duffy makes his home in an RV, signifying his ability to move both through Harlan and outside of the county into the larger spaces of Kentucky. The Crowe family in season 4 represent a different outside force. They also introduce another important element to the series, one not found in *The Wire*—the outsider's perspective. The Crowes have this, but so too does Raylon himself, having spent the last several years working in Miami before moving back to his home in Kentucky. His viewpoint gives us a unique sense of these characters and spaces, one that is simultaneously objective and subjective (see D. W. Winnicott); he both knows Harlan, in an intimate sense—his father, Arlo, for example, is caught up in the criminal underworld there—and maintains some level of distance both as a marshal and as a stranger.

Fargo too, has, in its first three seasons, offered a variety of different plot lines set in a variety of different times and places. To some extent *Fargo* works more like an "anthology" series than either *The Wire* or *Justified*. Specifically each season involves an entirely different crime and more specifically a slightly new space: Bemidji, Minnesota, in 2006, Luverne in 1979, and St. Cloud in 2010. They are united, however, by a few minor characters. Lou Solverson, for example, a primary investigator in season 2, is father to Molly Solverson the central police officer in season 1. More importantly, all three seasons, despite being set in different cities and time periods, are united by their atmosphere, one associated with the cold empty landscapes of the upper Midwest. As a result, the shift that occurs in each season only helps to expand that space, to push against its boundaries in the same way *The Wire* pushes into new neighborhoods.

Fargo explores its virtual world using many of the same techniques as these other series. We're given panoramic shots of the frozen tundra—god's-eye views. We travel highways at night with villain Lorne Malvo. Gus Grimley leaves his job as a policeman to become a postman, and only through his travels along snow-covered back roads does he finally discover the criminals' hideout. Central character Emmit Stussy in season 3 owns a chain of parking garages.

In addition, *Fargo* works hard to contrast its spaces in a way the other two series do not.

Drawing specifically on the landscape, the series emphasizes the wide open spaces of Minnesota, South Dakota, and North Dakota. Over and over again we're offered panoramic shots of this landscape, most often featured as snow-covered, empty, and lifeless. Such images highlight the relative isolation of the various locations within that larger wasteland. And the locations themselves, where the action occurs, are often spread out from one another. Lester Nygaard is kidnapped at one point and taken to a deserted frozen lake in the trunk of a car. Characters live in houses far from town and far from one another. Emmit Stussy's home in season 3, for instance, seems completely isolated from his neighbors. In addition, Stussy's parking decks, scattered all over the state, represent great vast empty spaces that seem to mirror the landscape of the upper Midwest. Another character from the third season, Ron Burgle, lives alone on a deserted stretch of road, and is actually killed when the murderer can't find the correct address in the wide uninhabited space of South Dakota; the murderer simply gets lost in the blank landscape and winds up at Burgle's by mistake. In fact, the episode in which he kills Burgle, the first episode of the season is appropriately titled, "The Law of Vacant Places."

With the individual spaces set so far apart, "paths" become especially important in *Fargo.* In the opening scene of the series, Malvo races along an empty highway. His lights show us little beyond the road's dividing lines, but as we see in the next scenes, set during the day, there is little to see. Bad things can happen in this wasteland. In this case, Malvo hits a deer and runs off the road; more sinister, as he sits dazed behind the wheel, the trunk pops open and a naked man flees into the woods. This moment is refigured in the first season's final episode. Frustrated as a cop, Gus Grimly has traded in his badge for a mail carrier's uniform, and we see him driving alone along empty

Figure 7.3. Wide open landscapes on Fargo.
***Fargo,* 1.1**

frozen back roads. Yet it is now, once he has taken a job traveling roads, when he finally finds the villains, spotting their car parked in front of an isolated cabin. Emmit Stussey meets his demise, at the end of season 3, on yet another deserted stretch of highway.

In contrast to the distance between locations, the interiors of the homes in the series are most often small, filled with too much furniture or awkwardly laid out. Lester Nygaard's house in the first season offers a useful illustration. In the first episode we find Lester in the basement, doing a bit of home repair on the family washing machine. The space is cramped, full of machines and storage boxes. When his wife Pearl enters, the space feels even smaller. She berates Lester, questioning his manhood and listing his many failings. Pearl is too close to Lester, too pressed into his space, and we can see on his face his desire to escape. The toolbox is too close to him as well, and in a moment of rage and frustration, Lester picks up a hammer and hits the looming Pearl squarely in the forehead, killing her. In another scene Lester meets the shady Lorne Malvo in a hospital waiting room. The seats are too close together, and too many people seem to walk by. As Malvo makes an illicit proposal to Lester, we feel Lester's discomfort. Malvo is too close, but at the same time Lester fears that someone in this crowded space will overhear their conversation. Parts of season 2 are set in Peggy and Ed Blumquist's cramped garage. The tiny space holds too many shadows, and in one, Ed discovers the man Peggy has hit with her car, the man she drove home with half in her windshield, the man Ed has no choice now but to murder, in part because there is simply not enough space in which to do anything else.

In the end all three shows contribute something important to television's development, its own sense of how its storyworlds work. If *The Wire* set the bar for using the police genre to complicate storyworld spaces, *Justified* and *Fargo* demonstrate that television continues to grow, continues to look for innovative methods of expanding and developing its spaces.

All three series share something else in common as well, though. All three are set in "real" locations—Baltimore; Harlan, Kentucky; and a handful of cities in the upper Midwest. All three, then, create fictional storyworld versions of real spaces. Obviously this doubling gives to the narratives a certain level of reality—*The Wire*, for example, filmed on Baltimore's city streets and many of the actors were former drug dealers or former police officers. But oddly the opposite can happen as well—the virtual world can sometimes leak out into the "real" world. Martin O'Malley, the "real" mayor of Baltimore at the time HBO broadcast the series, was a frequent critic, complaining it exaggerated the city's problems. For his part, creator David Simon has regularly criticized O'Malley, later governor of Maryland and presidential candidate, for having caused all the problems highlighted in the show.

One of the more interesting aspects of *The Wire* is its understanding of the relationship between these two spaces—virtual and real. From the first episode, it played with this relationship, searching for ways to confuse it. In virtually every episode, for example, the camera filters an image of a character through closed circuit TV or video surveillance of some sort. When McNulty enters the courthouse and passes through the metal detector, we see him on CCTV; the boys who run drugs in the pit are seen through a surveillance camera, throwing rocks at it until they've broken it; when McNulty takes his boys to the police station, leaving them in the lobby while he interrogates a subject, we see them through the video monitor that sits on the sergeant's desk. Meanwhile the wire itself serves to reduce the space of the city into nothing more than digital sound and images. As Detective Lester Freamon and Officer Beadie Russell monitor activity at the docks during season 2, the screen they watch looks like nothing so much as a video game, with cargo containers and semis turned into nothing more than avatars.

Finally, though, the final season of the series, season 5, made clear that nothing we saw on the show could be trusted. Reporter Scott Templeton's lies as a reporter cast doubt on the media—all media—including *The Wire* itself. But the fact that Templeton's lies are based on McNulty's elaborate invention of a serial killer terrorizing the homeless makes clear that, if the media can't be trusted, neither can reality. The series calls into question all that we know about Baltimore, all that we know about *The Wire*. It hints at its own artificiality. But it also bleeds out into the real world, suggesting that the real space of Baltimore is shaped by our images of Baltimore, images the show itself has spent five years creating.

Chapter 8

"These Are Their Stories"

Postmodern Spaces

If television—if art—aspires to virtual reality, to re-create the "real world," to offer us a "second life," what happens to reality itself when art succeeds? If, for example, we find ourselves able to enjoy an afternoon double-header at Wrigley Field simply by putting on a headset to experience the sights, sounds, and smells as if we were there, what becomes of the actual space of Wrigley Field? According to French philosopher Jean Baudrillard, in such a case, Wrigley Field—all of reality, in fact—becomes virtual. The VR experience is virtual; the real experience, with which the VR matches up in every possible sense, is virtual as well.

In *Simulacra and Simulation*, Baudrillard defines what he refers to as the "successive phases of the image" as we move closer to perfecting mimesis:

> it [the image] is a reflection of a profound reality;
> it masks and denatures a profound reality;
> it masks the *absence* of a profound reality;
> it has no relation to any reality whatsoever: it is its own pure simulacrum. (1994, 6).

What Baudrillard describes here is no less than the evolution of art as it approaches a level of verisimilitude such that we can no longer distinguish the artistic representation from the reality to which it refers. In the beginning the simulation is different enough from the simulated that we recognize them as distinct from one another. Eventually, however, the simulation reaches a point of perfection; it become indistinguishable from the real. In such a situation, the two become the same. To put things in terms of this book, the narrative becomes equivalent to "reality," or from another perspective, reality becomes as artificial as the narrative storyworld.

Baudrillard eventually came to see VR technology, computer simulations, as the ultimate source of the simulacrum, but for most of his career, the television was the device he associated with his phases of the image. In *Screened Out*, for example, he writes, "what if the sign did not relate to either object or meaning, but to the promotion of the sign as sign? And what if information did not relate either to the facts, but to the promotion of information itself as event? And more precisely today: what if television no longer related to anything except itself as message?" (2014, 188). In fact, this is exactly what television has succeeded in doing over the last thirty years—making TV the subject of TV. When TV no longer bears any relation "to any reality whatsoever," it is "its own pure simulacrum." At the same time as Marie-Laure Ryan argues in her gloss of Baudrillard, once we reach this point "we don't live in a world where there is something called VR technology; rather, we are immersed in this technology; we live and breathe virtual reality" (2015, 21): world equals storyworld.

The Wire understands this shift into the "postmodern." It recognizes that the more realistic a virtual space becomes, the more it turns the "real" spaces it originally only represented into virtual spaces as well. This explains why, in the final season, the show chose to turn the cameras on itself—using the newspaper as a metaphor for media broadly. Nothing is real, the season seems to proclaim, not the world we've created, but not the space of the "real" world either.

But finally, television raises yet one more question, one Baudrillard failed to consider. What happens when television understands postmodern theory? What happens when it becomes self-aware, when the show that *is* postmodern is also *about* postmodernism? In this chapter I try to offer some answers to these questions.

IMAGES OF IMAGES

Television hasn't always known it was a postmodern device, though even before Baudrillard it did sometimes seem to suspect. As the credits roll by during a second season episode of *Green Acres* ("I Didn't Raise My Pig to be a Solider"), Oliver and Lisa Douglas stare at them in disbelief; Lisa remarks, "Oliver, when I came out of the house there were some names in front of me." In a season 7 episode of *The Love Boat*, Florence Henderson and Robert Reed bump into one another at a breakfast buffet. The two are involved in different plotlines, but just for a moment Mr. and Mrs. Brady seem to recognize one another. Here the artificial reality is populated by artificial reality itself. Such moments draw attention to the fact that we are just watching a show, with actors who we recognize mostly from other shows. For the most part, though, until recently, television presented us with a portrayal of life and asked us to invest in it as reality. The world of *Father Knows Best* was meant to mirror the real world, and we were meant to suspend our disbelief and watch as though we were watching life unfold. That is, the television show "reflected a profound reality" or if we feel slightly more cynical "denature[d] a profound reality."

Once postmodern theory had explained what television was doing though, TV embraced its role. *St. Elsewhere* (1982–1987) was as much about other television shows as about specific medical cases or the personal lives of its doctors. Often, for instance, the PA system at St. Eligius would page doctors from other series. The producers created crossover episodes involving a number of other programs including *M*A*S*H* and *Cheers*. In later seasons, the character Elliot Carlin, originally a patient of psychologist Bob Hartley on *The Bob Newhart Show*, showed up in St. Eligius' psych ward.

Around the same time, Bob Newhart himself managed one of the greatest finales in television history when he had his character on *Newhart*, Dick Loudon wake up in the final moments of the show to discover he was back in his previous series, *The Bob Newhart Show*, now Robert Hartley sharing a bed with his wife Emily. *Cheers* frequently made reference to itself as in its meta-discussion of Shelly Long's departure mid-series. At a drive-in theater one night, Norm, Cliff, Frasier, and Woody discuss the *Godzilla* franchise: "Isn't that the part usually played by Akira Nakamura?" Cliff asks. "Yeah," Norm replies, "but she left half way through the *Godzilla* series." "I don't understand," Woody says from the backseat, "Why would an actress leave right in the middle of a successful series?" In the midst of a *3rd Rock from the Sun* episode ("Tricky Dick"), John Lithgow suddenly becomes carried away and the fiery minister he played in *Footloose* emerges. In all of these examples, the fictional space of the show isn't meant to reference the real world but rather other narrative storyworlds.

It's Garry Shandling's Show (1986–1990) raised self-reference to another level altogether. The show proclaimed itself to be about itself. Shandling spent a good part of each episode speaking directly to the audience, not merely breaking the fourth wall but recognizing them as an audience and reminding them at every turn they were watching a sitcom. "So I want to tell you all what's going on in my life," he tells them in the first two minutes of the first episode, "but first I've got to go to the bathroom. You can watch the opening credits and I should be right back." The soundstage on which Garry's home was built was one and the same with the soundstage on which the series was filmed. Even the theme song was about itself: "This is the theme to Garry's show, This is the theme to Garry's show, Garry called me up and asked if I would write his theme song. I'm almost half way finished, how do you like it so far?"

By the 2000s, the airwaves seemed full of shows not just making reference to other pop culture "images," but wholly based on pop culture. *30 Rock*, a show about making a show, featured plotlines in which Liz Lemon hallucinates a meeting with Oprah and shows up for jury duty dressed as Princess Leia. During the second season, the show promoted "Green Week" by having the show within the show satirically promote Green Week. *Community* regularly turned episodes into extended homages to *M*A*S*H*, *Doctor Who*, and Christmas Claymation specials. In "Cooperative Calligraphy," the show presents a "bottle episode," during which Abed repeatedly reminds everyone they are in a "bottle episode," pointing out each characteristic of such episodes as it occurs. Shandling himself went on to create *The Larry Sanders Show*, in which he plays a late night talk show host; guests in each episode are actors playing outsized versions of themselves: David Duchovny appears as David Duchovny, an image referencing his own pop star image. On *Psych* Shawn and Gus reference pop culture characters, spout famous quotes, and reunite the cast of *Twin Peaks*. And this list doesn't include the musical episodes that began appearing near the end of series runs—*Psych*, *Buffy the Vampire Slayer*, *Once Upon a Time* have all featured one. In these episodes the cast simply discard all pretense to reality, breaking into spontaneous song and dance while simultaneously expressing their own amazement at their storyworld having turned suddenly "artificial."

Perhaps *Family Guy* has done the most to recapture the original spirit of *It's Garry Shandling's Show*. In the episode "Back to the Pilot," for example, Stewie and Brian use Stewie's time machine to travel back in time to the first episode of the series—the pilot. Here again, the subject of the episode becomes another episode: the content of the new episode essentially the same as the content of the original. Brian and Stewie are simply drawn over the animation that already exists, literally made to occupy the space they already occupied. Additionally, the two make observations about this space: they draw attention to a change in Meg's voice for instance, the result of a change in the actress playing the role (from Lacey Chabert to Mila Kunis) that occurred after the first season; they point out a flaw in the animation, a place where Peter's eye is drawn over his glasses. They discuss one of *Family Guy*'s tropes—the cutaway—and set up a joke about what the family actually does during the cutaways. The joke relies on treating the family in the show as "real," despite the fact they are animated. But in order for the joke to work as a joke, we must recognize the artificiality of the show. That is, if we buy into the animated characters as "real" flesh-and-blood actors, then it makes sense to wonder what they do during cutaways. Only if we know they are animated is the joke funny. In other words, the joke treats the show as "reality," while at the same time undermining that reality.

However, all of these self-references and meta-narratives create a certain amount of confusion if we return to Baudrillard's "phases of the image." In particular, does a show about itself belong to his third or fourth phase? On the one hand, when characters comment on the opening credits as they stream by, it serves to pull us out of the show's world, reminding us that world isn't real. For Baudrillard, that effect should reinforce the notion that our own world is real. Reality disappears during the third phase, but crucially, we continue to believe it exists: the image "masks the *absence* of a profound reality." The key word here is "mask": the image itself manages to convince us reality remains even after it is gone. Baudrillard famously uses Disneyland to illustrate his point, arguing that Disneyland as a place feels so absolutely artificial that when we leave we are reassured that the world outside is "real": "Disneyland is presented as imaginary in order to make us believe that the land presented as imaginary is real, whereas all of Los Angeles and the America that surrounds it are no longer real" (1994, 12). Feeling reality's loss, we search for it desperately, but it no longer exists, and our desperation to find it only makes us all the more susceptible to being drawn in by the artificial.

But crucially, such shows as *Family Guy* and *Community* also undermine reality by refusing to reference it, by referencing themselves instead. At the same time, they teach us to see the real world through a television lens, to interpret the events in our lives through those we've seen on TV. In this sense, such shows simultaneously erase the world and "mask" the world's disappearance. The stronger the virtual world TV creates, the more that virtual reality undermines reality itself, and the more TV comes to regard itself as "reality." Television both *is* postmodern in this sense and *comments* on postmodernism, which is itself a postmodern act—one enormous postmodern feedback loop.

It seems as though the blatant artificiality of shows like *Community* and especially *Seinfeld* (see below) helped spawn a kind of backlash in 2000, driven by a deep longing for the "real." In the wake of such shows and their deeply artificial spaces, audiences went in search of the real. Initially, at least, they found it in *Survivor*, and specifically in the seemingly everyday behaviors of a group of randomly chosen strangers thrown together and struggling to survive in a "real" space. The reality gameshow, however, involved some obvious manipulation; as a result it couldn't maintain its status as "reality" for long. Not that this diminished the popularity of such shows. In fact, they only increased in number, with powerhouse programs like *Big Brother*, *American Idol*, and *The Bachelor* coming on the heels of *Survivor*'s success.

But part of the entertainment value in watching such shows was not in investing in them as real, but in seeking out the artificial. And like television's version of *Disneyland*, our recognition managed to convince us, for a bit longer anyway, that our real world was still "real."

The result has been a succession of reality TV genres, each new wave of shows laying claim to "reality," and each ultimately being revealed as artificial. We have seen the likes of *Iron Chef*, *Mythbusters*, *The Dog Whisperer*, *Dance Moms*, *The Real Housewives*, *Jon and Kate Plus 8*, and *Little People, Big World* come and go. Each new version of "reality"—the expose, the historical documentary, the close examination of an everyday person's "real life"—eventually revealed itself as artificial. The more we came to understand the power of editing to shape the stories we saw, or that producers might use outright manipulation to encourage character behaviors or manufacture conflict, the more the television reality seemed to slip from our grasp, but the more life seemed real.

TRUE OR FALSE?

I conclude this chapter with two very different, though equally important examples of how television has further confused the real world with the storyworld.

The first of these involves the popular and critically acclaimed sitcom, *Seinfeld.* Oddly enough, despite the fact it was a sitcom, the show was originally based in reality, with Jerry Seinfeld looking to parley his standup career into a series. The original format of the show drew parallels between his standup and his life, as though his life fed his standup, or—in a postmodern sense—perhaps his standup became the source for his life. Certainly the standup bits featured at the beginning and end of each episode seemed to set up the events that were to follow. We might be encouraged to think of those events as fuel for the jokes then, but structurally the jokes actually set up the events. In this sense the show was more "real" than say *The Bob Newhart Show* or *Home Improvement*, other comedian-centered vehicles that situated the comedian in a different reality—psychologist or handyman. Jerry was a comedian playing a comedian. Additionally, Seinfeld drew on many of the real aspects of his life in putting the show together. Famously the character of George Costanza was based on Seinfeld's writing partner and the show's co-creator Larry David, while Cosmo Kramer was based on Kenny Kramer, a one-time neighbor of David's in New York.

The show itself became famous for being about nothing but that wasn't quite true. In fact, *Seinfeld* was about sitcoms. That is, it mined the traditional sitcom format, utilizing the tropes of a sitcom world but pushing them as far as they could be stretched, and beyond this point into absurdity. It offered four stereotypical characters, characters who rather than grow and develop as the series went on, only seemed to become more stereotypical. It played with the traditional formula of wrapping an episode up neatly at the end by having the various strands of an episode—no matter how far flung from one another—almost magically come together in the end. In one episode, for example, Kramer heads to the beach to hit golf balls; meanwhile, George pretends to be a marine biologist in order to impress a woman. Though the two plotlines bear no relationship to one another, in the end we discover George saved a beached whale whose blowhole happened, coincidentally, to be blocked by one of Kramer's golf balls. The show worked deliberately to create catch-phrases, reveling in its own ability to invent ridiculous phrases that caught on: "close talker"; "man hands"; "sponge-worthy." And it played with conventions of location and time, with episodes that took place entirely in one location, such as a Chinese restaurant or a parking garage, and episodes in which events took place in reverse order. In fact, the show's deconstruction of the sitcom genre proved so thorough that for some years after its final episode, critics declared the genre dead (see, for example, *Entertainment Weekly*'s 1999 article, "The Death of the Sitcom"). Not until 2005 did *The Office*—a series that pretended to be "real" footage—find success by pretending to offer reality.

Then, in season 4, the producers had Seinfeld, the character, write a pilot for *Seinfeld*, the show. The result was another instance of crossed worlds similar to that in *Family Guy*'s "Pilot." On the one hand, this move served to heighten the show's realism in that, like other elements of the show, it drew on real events from Seinfeld's life, particularly his effort with Larry David to create a sitcom. And yet this element drawn from real life also served to undercut the show's authenticity. As we watch Jerry and George make the pilot, we are forced to recognize that what we were watching—the show itself—is no more real than the show they make during the episode.

The remainder of the series and its afterlife only heightened the confusion between the real and the fictional. First, as the show continued its run, fans began to explore its underlying reality. That is, visitors to New York began looking for the locations, filmic and real, used in the series. This reached a climax when Kenny Kramer, the model for the character, began giving bus tours of these locations, tours that he dubbed "The *Seinfeld* Reality Tour." Not to be outdone, *Seinfeld* producers wrote this into their own plotline, with the character Kramer selling his personal stories to clothing mogul J. Peterman, and then to make money offering the "J. Peterman Reality" bus tour of locations from his life.

The tangle of fiction and reality became even more bizarre when Larry David began his next project, a "reality show" in which cameras followed him in his "real" life, a ruse designed to give his scripted show—like *The Office*—a realistic flavor. Over the course of the series David repeatedly tries to work with one or another of his *Seinfeld* colleagues on new creative projects, projects that inevitably fall through (even as the show itself becomes those projects). Then, in an inspired piece of writing, David decided to stage a *Seinfeld* reunion episode, involving all of the original cast. The principles reunited and filmed themselves filming a reunion episode, but of course this was in the context of a "fake" reality show, meaning the *reality* was that the entire reunion was scripted and staged. In short, David managed to create both a simulated reunion and an actual reunion. The "world,"—the space we saw—worked as both.

Seinfeld provides an example of a fictional show occasionally crossing over into reality. My second example offers the opposite: an example of an apparently real program that in fact turned out to be complete fiction. The Animal Planet's 2011 special, *Mermaids: the Body Found* was set up to resemble documentary, with purported found footage, a deep-voiced narrator, and testimony from the scientists who were involved in recovering a mermaid corpse. And in fact, *Mermaids* referenced some real events, including a mass whale beaching and an unexplained underwater sound known popularly as the "bloop" originally detected by the National Oceanic and Atmospheric Administration (NOAA) in 1997. The "scientists," however, were in fact actors; the story they told was fictional; the footage of two teenage boys discovering a mermaid caught in nets was entirely manufactured; and the "theory" upon which the show was based, the "aquatic ape theory," is speculative at best. Yet not only did the network and the producers fail to label the show as "fiction," they actually went to some lengths to confuse viewers into believing the story was real. Part of their efforts involved mixing "real phenomenon" such as the bloop and the beached whales with the fiction, without clearly distinguishing between the two. But the producers used more deliberate tricks as well. At one point, for instance, we're shown footage that is clearly labeled at the bottom of the screen as "recreated." The inclusion of such footage, using actors who portray the scientists (who in fact are themselves actors), suggests—as with Baudrillard's Disneyland—that the rest of what we see is "real." Additionally, Animal Planet went so far as to set up a fake web page for one of the show's "scientists," which it then blocked, replacing the page's content with a warning from a government agency that the original page had been taken down for unspecified violations. In interviews about the program, producer Charlie Foley carefully avoided calling his work "fiction," choosing instead to label it a "story," and offering ambiguous statements such as, "If that theory were true, and humans were once becoming marine mammals but we stopped evolving in that direction, it made me wonder: what if one group never stopped evolving in that direction? Could there be an evolutionary basis for a legendary creature? That was the starting point for the story" (2013, n.p.). The channel's intent was apparently

Figure 8.1. Scientists in a submarine capture video evidence of mermaids. ***Mermaids: the New Evidence***

not to create a "mockumentary," or explore the conventions of the documentary genre, but rather to present itself as reality.

Mermaids: The Body Found was followed two years later by *Mermaids: The New Evidence*. If anything, this second program created even more confusion between reality and fiction. Much of the show took place in a studio, with a real host—Jon Frankel—discussing the events with the fictional scientist from the first film. Midway through the program, we're shown footage of an unidentified, blurry creature sunning itself on rocks before quickly sliding into the sea. The footage was purportedly taken by college students visiting a town in Israel, and the footage appears on YouTube labeled as such, though whether it is genuine or placed there by Animal Planet is unclear. Furthermore, the broadcast includes a CNN report on the Israeli town of Kiryat Yam and its mayor who apparently offered a $1,000,000 reward for video proof of mermaids. The mayor is apparently real, and he appears on the program and comments on the footage, but whether he is genuinely commenting on real footage, genuinely commenting on fake footage, or in on the fiction is also unclear. Finally, at the show's end, we're shown "new footage," taken from inside a deep sea submarine, of what appears to be a mermaid streaking by the sub's window and pressing her mermaid hand to it. While clearly manufactured, the footage resembles in great detail the footage of a giant squid captured for the first time on film at roughly the same time as the "mermaids" and featured in an apparently genuine documentary, with an equally sensational title, *Monster Squid: The Giant is Real* broadcast on Animal Planet's sister network, Discovery.

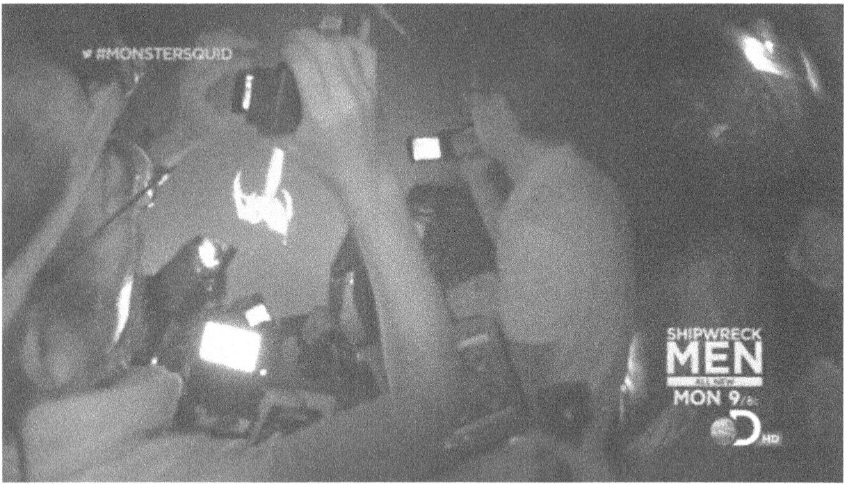

Figure 8.2. Scientists in a submarine capture video evidence of giant squid.
Monster Squid: The Giant is Real

In the end, though, how different is such a fictional documentary from so-called "speculative" documentaries—*Finding Bigfoot*, *Ancient Aliens*, *Ghost Adventures*—which appear on the same networks: Animal Planet, the History Channel, the Travel Channel? Simply by appearing on such networks they are given an aura of genuineness. Experts appear above lengthy labels that seem to provide respectable credentials, as in *Ancient Aliens*: "Publisher of *Legendary Times* Magazine"; "Founding Curator of the Joseph Campbell Archives." The reality of what we see is only further muddied by the appearance of scientific experts who testify to actual science that is then used to make a case for speculative theories.

Yet to criticize such programs as "fake" only puts us back in the position of trying to reinvest the real world with reality. Even if we examine a relatively faithful documentary such as *An American Family*, which appeared on PBS in 1973, reality is undone, replaced with storyworld. Such a program cannot possibly show all of its footage, so it must necessarily edit that footage, picking and choosing events, rendering its reality suspect. But more important than this aspect of all film and photography, the intrusion of the camera itself into the Loud family's space disrupted that space. Almost immediately, cracks began appearing in their relationships. These were apparently exacerbated by the strain of the filming process to the point that what we wound up witnessing was the dissolution of the Loud's marriage. PBS set out to create "reality" television, but wound up broadcasting a narrative storyworld.

After the broadcast, the Louds themselves complained that the raw footage had been edited to bring out the worst aspects of their personalities and behaviors. Television's intrusion into these people's real lives had turned them into characters for the audience, but it also made them characters to themselves. Again in a fiction-reality feedback loop the family's real lives were shaped by having been filmed for television, television then shaped the footage to create characters, and the impact of that editing ultimately further changed their "real" personalities.

Similar events have occurred in relation to more recent series. Jon and Kate Gosselin divorced in the midst of their successful series *Jon and Kate Plus 8*. Likewise, Matt and Amy Roloff divorced in the middle of *Little People, Big World*. Meanwhile, Josh Duggar, of *19 Kids and Counting* was revealed to have molested his sisters. Not all of these events can be blamed on television of course; what is clear, though, is that in each case what we saw on television didn't simply remain on television but rather burst the bounds of the screen to affect our attitudes and opinions toward what were ostensibly real events, draining them of their reality.

It seems, then, that in the end, we are left with the fact that no matter which way we turn, television spaces have fundamentally altered the real world. The question we are left with at the end of this chapter is what constitutes the real world and what constitutes the "narrative" world. Or are they simply one and the same? To return again to Marie-Laure Ryan, maybe "we don't live in a world where there is something called VR technology; rather, we are immersed in this technology; we live and breathe virtual reality" (2015, 21).

One of the interesting consequences of this question is that it undoes the distinction between television and VR as separate media forms. That is, while VR (that is, computer-generated simulation) sometimes threatens to outpace television as our primary source of entertainment, and for that matter to replace our world entirely, perhaps the shift to a virtual reality has already occurred. Perhaps television is the true "virtual reality" or at least the device through which we have achieved it.

Chapter 9

"On the Next *Arrested Development*"

Of TV Endings

As we might expect, the Western, in whatever its media form, has always been about space. In the nineteenth century, western America was a space to be explored, a new space to be inhabited, a space to be conquered and controlled, and the novels and films about this period of American expansion generally emphasize space and movement into and within it. Recent series *Westworld*, however, offers a fresh take on the genre, though, one that is uniquely tied to television. As with other series I have examined in this book, it pushes its spatial boundaries in ways a novel or film simply can't. But additionally, it offers an important commentary on how television, in a postmodern sense, has managed to make all of reality into a virtual space.

In the same way *The Wire* sets up to be a traditional police drama, *Westworld* sets up to be a traditional Western. Central character Teddy arrives not insignificantly, for instance, by rail, the train carving a path into this empty landscape as it takes him into town. However, as we soon discover, all is not what it seems.

It begins strangely: a naked young woman sits slumped on a chair in the dark. Two disembodied voices, a man and a woman—her name is Delores; his is not revealed—discuss the nature of dreams and reality. The camera slowly zooms in on the figure, and the lights come up to reveal a glass-enclosed room, sterile and with hard edges: this room belongs to the future. The woman remains motionless, expressionless. Nothing moves in the room—or almost nothing: a single housefly crawls over her face—across her forehead, down her nose. When at last it crawls over her eyeball we know for certain: this body is empty and lifeless.

But then something more familiar. On screen, a young woman (the same young woman, in fact) lies in bed, her eyes fluttering open on a new day. We watch her walk down the stairs of a rustic home wearing an old-fashioned floor-length dress. She greets her father, a grizzled man who sits ruminating over his cup of coffee on the front porch, before she heads off, easel in hand, to "set down some of this natural splendor." We see shots of Monument Valley; an old-time player piano begins to crank out a wobbly tune: if the opening scenes belong to the future, these scenes belong to the past, specifically the American West, circa 1870.

Cut to another scene: a young man with rugged good looks stares out the window of a train onto that same Monument Valley as the train makes its way to a dusty little frontier town. It rolls into the station, a mass of steam. The man steps off the platform and makes his way past a host of Western stereotypes—children tormenting the town drunk; the sherriff forming a posse to head up into the hills after outlaws. He walks to the local saloon, where he and the barkeep go through a ritual familiar to us from Western films:

> "Rye whiskey."
> "What about it?"
> "Well it ain't doing any good sittin' in that bottle."

In the next scene the two main characters—Delores and Teddy—meet up with one another, and we quickly discover from their dialogue that this is not their first encounter:

> "You came back."
> "I told you I would."

On horseback the two chase one another playfully through the picturesque landscape of rust colored buttes and patches of scrub brush until, near sundown, they perch on a hill above a herd of cattle. Delores explains to Teddy about the Judas steer, the one the rest of the herd follows: "I forget you dress like a cowboy but that's about the extent of it."

The couple arrive back at the homestead after sunset, but something is wrong: the cattle have not yet been put away for the night. Teddy rushes ahead to find bandits have attacked the house and murdered Delores's parents. Wasting no time, he dispatches all three ruffians, but the damage has been done: when Delores arrives, all she can do is cradle her father's head in her arms.

But then more strangeness. Another bandit steps out of the darkness, this one different from the others, more self-assured, more menacing. This time, when Teddy tries to face the bad guy down, he finds his bullets are useless. Even at point blank range, they have no effect. Instead, after some talk of metaphysics and existentialism, talk that reminds us of the sterile room from the beginning of the episode, this dark stranger kills Teddy with ease.

Bending down, he grabs Delores by her hair, and drags her into the barn, the whole miserable scene reflected in Teddy's now lifeless eye (an echo of Delores's dead eye with which we began).

And so the little drama draws to a close. Except that it doesn't. Instead, in the next shot we return to Delores lying comfortably in bed, her eyes opening just as before on a new day. The rickety piano starts up again. We see Teddy arriving on the same train, looking out the same window at the same landscape. This time, though, the camera pulls back, giving us a shot of the train from above, a shot that pulls even further back, until the train seems only a toy, until the landscape itself seems a plaything, until at last we see the entire "world" stretched out beneath us, laid out upon a platform surrounded by technicians with clipboards.

In this moment, the two halves of what we've seen make sense for the first time. Teddy, Delores, the town, the whole landscape: none of them are "real." Instead, they are all part of a carefully designed, carefully monitored virtual simulation of a frontier community. As the episode continues, we learn more about the nature of this simulation: Westworld is a kind of vacation resort, a playground where real humans participate in carefully scripted adventures in a simulation of the Old West populated by lifelike robots—Delores, Teddy, the sheriff, and the barkeep. Visitors to the park can help hunt down outlaws, or spend time in local brothels, or duel black-hatted bad guys on Main Street. Behind the scenes, a massive corporation keeps the whole experience running

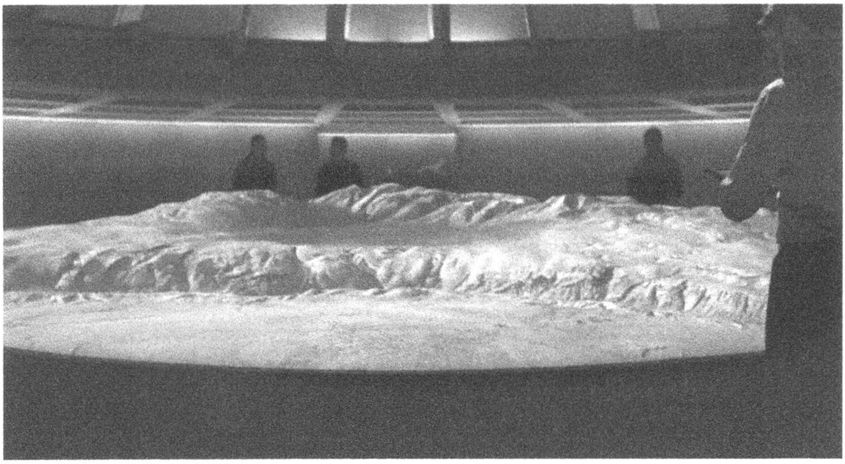

Figure 9.1. All of Westworld, seen as a hologram by the technicians who run it. *Westworld,* 1.1

smoothly, making adjustments here and there when a robot malfunctions or a plot needs tweaking.

TELEVISION'S VR ANXIETY

In some ways, *Westworld* works as a model for television. It is an elaborate storyworld, one its guests—its audience—enter and explore. It is an imagined space that we enter through a path, in this case the railroad. And while it does offer a number of pre-determined storylines that guide its visitors in particular directions, it is also possible to simply explore those spaces, to push beyond their boundaries and discover new corners of the world.

In a postmodern sense, though, the storyworld is also threatening to move outside the boundaries of the park itself. Delores, Teddy, and others of the AI characters, have begun to realize who and what they are, and are beginning to search for ways to break out of their roles, break out of the storyworld altogether and invade the "real" world. Perhaps even more significant, one of the park's employees, Bernard Lowe, doesn't know he is an AI. This, more than the characters becoming self-aware, calls into question the entire notion of "real" and "artificial." It suggests that no one can really know if they inhabit a real space or a virtual one; we must all assume then, that our world is virtual.

But while Westworld is its own storyworld, *Westworld* is a storyworld itself, one we explore. It is a storyworld within a storyworld. And as a fantasy of the future, a glimpse of increasingly complex simulations, artificial spaces that seem so real even the characters within them don't know they themselves are not real—in that sense the show offers a kind of warning about the future of entertainment. It expresses TV's own anxiety about what these new sorts of entertainment might mean for television's own future.

In fact, TV seems to be thinking a lot about such alternative realities these days and thinking about them with some anxiety. The technologies that drive these simulations come in many different forms. In the *Westworld* version, "real" humans explore a "real" space, but a space carefully crafted to resemble a time and place that no longer exist, and a space populated by artificial, if lifelike, humans. The small Idaho town in FOX's recent series *Wayward Pines* offers a similar façade, though in this case the simulation has nothing to do with "play." Over the course of season 1 of the series, FBI agent Ethan Burke struggles to learn the truth about Wayward Pines, a town from which he can't seem to escape, a town surrounded by enormous concrete walls, where those who question the authorities are hanged. Eventually, he learns the year is 4014 not 2014. Man has been replaced in the evolutionary chain by humanoid creatures known as "Abbies." The town itself was originally designed to keep survivors from learning the horrifying truth—that they are a tiny oasis of mankind in a world where they no longer belong. Those who discover that truth, who see the simulation for what it is, risk going mad.

Other shows conceive of virtual reality in different terms. Syfy's *Battlestar Galactica* prequel, *Caprica* revolves around the invention of a digital second life that, as in *Westworld*, serves as a kind of playground for those bored with reality. In this case, however, the simulation involves direct mental projections through the use of sophisticated gaming glasses known as holobands. No robots or constructed buildings here; instead, the characters enter a more intense level of "real," one apparently experienced neurologically (though this world does come with certain limitations: participants are protected, for instance, from actually dying in this space). In the second season of CBS's series *Under the Dome*, the townspeople are held in stasis, trapped in a cave underground. The events they experience are only a shared dream, another sort of mental projection, in this case controlled by alien technology. In an episode of *Black Mirror* from season 3, "San Junipero," the characters visit computer-generated versions of past eras—the 1980s, the 1990s—in their minds. They can choose to inhabit these digital spaces permanently at the end of their lives, essentially extending their lives forever. In "Extremis" from *Doctor Who*'s tenth season, the Bill and Doctor we follow through the episode eventually discover they are only digital images—copies of the originals—in a hologram designed (again, by aliens) to test out possible ways to conquer the Earth.[1] Other examples of the virtual on television include *The Dollhouse*, *Community*, *Mr. Robot*, *Legion*, *Lost*, and *Marvel's Agents of S.H.I.E.L.D.* Sometimes the virtual offers hope for a better life; other times its arrival heralds a dark dystopia where humankind loses its identity or its freedom or both. The differences matter less here than the fascination itself.[2] But this begs the question: Where does this relatively recent fascination originate?

The simplest answer has to do with the development of technology itself. Westworld may not exist, but what once seemed like the stuff of science fiction—robots, and holodecks, and artificial intelligence—has finally arrived, at least in primitive forms. The Oculus Rift, a headset that allows wearers to visually inhabit a simulated space, one they can enter and walk about in, appeared on the market in early 2016. It was followed quickly by similar devices from Sony, HTC, Samsung, and Google. On the content side of VR, more and more "experiences" are being developed to take advantage of headset technologies. *USAToday* online, for example, now features "Virtually There," a series of virtual "experiences"—roller coaster rides, professional bullfighting, even illegal Mexican border crossings—available to anyone with the right equipment.

As visual technologies continue to develop, other companies are at work improving the physical experience through haptic feedback systems. Nintendo Switch's Joy-Con controllers have already introduced a video game "rumble" feature, which simulates the feeling of holding, manipulating, and using objects: "one of the minigames included in launch title 1–2 Switch tasks players with guessing how many virtual balls are inside one of the Joy-Cons. It provided a surprisingly accurate rumble sensation that allows players to accurately guess the number of virtual items" (Porter 2017, n.p.). Other companies are busy designing so-called haptic vests and even whole suits that allow users to experience a holographic simulation with their entire bodies. And the Virtuix company is working on a VR platform that promises "physical experiences like walking and running" in digital environments (2017, n.p.).

But not only will the platforms feel real in the future; they will allow us more and more "agency," or control over the virtual environment. Advances in computer processing power and the promise of such technologies as the quantum computer, suggest true artificial intelligence may soon be within our grasp. Google, for instance, which is busy developing quantum computing in a joint project with NASA, refers to its work as "quantum artificial intelligence." (Basulto 2015, n.p.). But even without quantum computing, AI has made enormous advances in recent years. Self-driving cars, for instance, have already been legalized in Florida and Michigan, while a host of other states, including California, have laws that allow these vehicles to be tested on the road. A simulation's ability to anticipate our next moves and create new landscapes, new experiences as real time responses, would make the simple visual experience of an Oculus Rift exponentially more lifelike.

And what of the possibility of direct neurological experiences as in *Caprica*? From a biological perspective, our ability to experience virtual feelings through our nervous system are also coming closer to reality. British engineer Kevin Warwick, for example, managed in 2002 to connect his own nervous system to his wife's and experience directly her hand and arm movements (2014, n.p). Warwick has also fused rat brain cells with robotic technology, creating "living" machines capable of learning to navigate simple spaces on their own (Delvin 2008, n.p.). And scientists at the J. Craig Venter Institute have apparently managed to "design life from scratch" through synthetic cells containing artificial DNA (Callaway 2016, n.p.).

Such tantalizing glimpses of a world to come, a world in which artificial realities might truly become indistinguishable from our real lives, where, like the characters in Westworld or some of the cylons in *Battlestar Galactica*, we might not actually know what is real and what is simulation, raise important questions. How will we utilize these new technologies and the new "spaces" they create? How will such technologies change us? Are we really in danger of losing our ability to distinguish between the artificial and the real? Will these artificial worlds offer us utopias in which we can choose our own race, our own gender, adopt superpowers, and eliminate physical labor; or a dystopia, where computer systems control what we do and who we are, eliminating the very essence of what makes us human? With questions like these more culturally central than ever, television offers an important outlet for positing answers.

But television's obsession with alternative realities has a deeper explanation as well. If Westworld, the amusement park, represents a media revolution, an entirely new way to interact with the world, both the real world and those simulations of it we can imagine, what does this revolution mean for the future of television? How exactly will programs on the Travel Channel compete with our ability to put on a pair of glasses and walk virtually on a beach in Jamaica? What will become of shows like *ER*, when we can stand in a virtual operating room with the surgeons, or perhaps even perform the surgery ourselves? Seen in this way, series like *Westworld* and *Wayward Pines* and *Legion* aren't simply television imagining a future; in such series, television—a technology for telling stories—thinks about the future of storytelling technologies. In doing so, TV expresses a deep anxiety about its own future, a fear of being replaced.

THE TROUBLE WITH ENDINGS

To borrow a phrase, television especially abhors an ending. As I argued in chapter 1, television derives much of its force from its seriality, and seriality presupposes a never-ending narrative, a limitless landscape. Perhaps this helps explain why fans are so routinely disappointed in series finales. In point of fact, we don't want our shows to end. Each spring, as networks begin thinking over their fall schedules, the same processes start over again, with loyal viewers mounting last minute campaigns to save their favorite low-rated series from the chopping block. When shows are cancelled the inevitable gnashing of teeth begins, the stages of grief, with bargaining—is there still time to find another network to pick it up?—chief among them. And when they do inevitably draw to a close, we're never quite satisfied with the endings. Fans still complain about the last episode of *Seinfeld*. Debates rage over how *The Sopranos* came to a close. In fact, the producers of *Battlestar Galactica* and *Lost* have both admitted that they had no clear ending in mind when they began their series. Ronald Moore notes of *Battlestar*:

> I think it hangs together better than it has any right to. I do feel good that the process I always believed in and really defended—about feeling the story

> instinctively as you go through it and not being tied to "Oh, we know exactly how it's going to end up"—that that was true [. . .]. There's loose threads and things that don't quite work, but I think that's in the nature of almost any new show. By and large I think we did a pretty good job of it. (Sepinwall 2009, n.p.)

Rumors have always circulated the *Lost*'s producers made things up as they went along. Nick Santora, a writer for the series *Prison Break*, reports a conversation he had with *Lost* writers. When asked how they planned to wrap up the many wild storylines they had already created, the answer was simple: "We're not. We literally just think of the weirdest [. . .] thing and write it and we're never going to pay it off" (Hooten 2015, n.p.). This kind of approach makes sense in regards to serial storytelling, where the goal is not to create a structurally sound narrative but rather one that can continue on indefinitely, even if that means endings may ultimately leave us disappointed. In proper postmodern fashion, *Arrested Development* used to end episodes with a preview of the upcoming episode, a preview that was entirely invented and had nothing, in fact, to do with any future episodes. This continued right up to the final episode after the show had been cancelled, in which we were given a preview of "the epilogue," a nod to series' open-endedness.

But what of television's own ending? Computer generated VR, digitally based simulations certainly seem like the logical next step in the evolution of storyworld technology. As I have suggested, even television itself seems to view such technologies as a threat. It turns out, in fact, that this question is connected to television's inability to offer satisfactory conclusions. If seriality prevents TV series from ending well, it also suggests television itself might not be easy to supplant.

Marie-Laure Ryan writes of these "coming" technologies that from the very beginning they were less about substance and more about "a grand flourish of rhetoric." More importantly, she calls into question the radical claims for such technologies as the Oculus Rift as generally overblown. In particular, she points out that for the moment, digital VR experiences don't engage our whole body: "Though VR is widely credited with the power to create a richer and more diversified environment than any other medium, its potential contribution to the expansion of the sensory dimensions of an image is really quite limited" (2015, 41). Headsets, for instance, only re-create a visual image, and while they do so in immersive three dimensions, these images aren't exactly an enormous leap forward from a painting, a film, or a TV episode. Additionally, she suggests that a truly immersive digital simulation will involve "unmediated presence," the disappearance of the hardware and software from our realm of perception, a point that, for the moment, seems well beyond our technological grasp.

In *Television Is the New Television*, Michael Wolff goes further than Ryan in taking digital media to task and extolling TV's staying power: "For sixty years, television, given massive generational, behavioral, and technological shifts, has managed to change . . . not so much (the world still sits in front of a television). And yet it is always, no matter its continued success, ubiquity, and cultural centrality, about to be swept away" (2015, chapter 3). In fact, Wolff argues, recent digital advancements have only further entrenched television as a medium. He writes compellingly, for instance, of Netflix's effect on the balance of power between TV and the digital universe: "It is not Netflix bringing digital to television, but, quite obviously, Netflix bringing television programming and values and behavior—like passive watching—to heretofore interactive and computer-related screens" (2015, chapter 11).

How exactly do the prophets of the digital revolution have it so wrong then? The answer can be found by examining the evolution of artistic media. The history of art is a history of advancements in realism. Each new advancement fundamentally startles our senses. This is the source of the—perhaps apocryphal—story of the Lumiere brothers' first exhibitions. As the tale goes, when they showed film of trains arriving at a station, audience members actually jumped out of the way, believing the train to be real. Such is our response to new media experiences: they so startle us we take them momentarily for real. But as the history of film demonstrates, the mind quickly adjusts to these new experiences, learns how to read the new media. In short, VR headsets may seem to offer a radical new experience, but the truth is, once we adjust to the visual world they offer, it isn't so very startling after all.

In fact, many of the technologies on the horizon, technologies that seem to threaten television's reign, may ultimately turn out to be advances in television rather than replacements, as Wolff's Netflix example illustrates. Many of the grim prognostications about television, in fact, have to do with shifts in how we access content. The fact that many people have begun to "cut the cord," using online services to view their shows rather than cable companies is the same thing as declaring TV itself dead. Television isn't defined however by its container, the means through which it is conveyed, or the device on which it appears. If that were true, television might be said to have ended when the console went out of style. The history of television has seen many changes, from the addition of color, to the expansion of cable, to the production and distribution of entire seasons on DVD, to the invention of the DVR, to the arrival of services like Hulu and Netflix. But if we define television based on its seriality and immediacy, as indeed I have tried to do in this book, none of these changes can be said to have "replaced" television, only altered some of the ways we consume it. Neither will a device like the VR headset, at least not in the short term. Such devices will need content.

If indeed a new narrative medium does exist on the horizon, one capable of replacing television, it certainly won't do so soon. For one thing, new technology takes time to develop, to learn its own strengths and define its own abilities. As I have tried to point out in this book, television took over fifty years to fully understand its own capabilities. In the meantime, new technologies will continue to make use of the old. McLuhan points out, the content of any medium is always "another medium": "The content of writing is speech, just as the written word is the content of print and print is the content of the telegraph" (1964, 23–24). Drawing on McLuhan, Bolter and Grusin use the term "remediation," which they define as taking content "from one medium and using it in another" (2000, 45). New technologies, in their formulation, always rely on remediation for their initial content. And Henry Jenkins notes, "history teaches us that old media never die—and they don't even necessarily fade away. What dies are simply the tools we use to access media content—the 8 track, the Beta tape" (2007, 13). At present, devices like the Oculus Rift offer very little of their own content. The most likely scenario for widespread use of this and similar headset technologies is that they will simply plug in previous content or develop roughly equivalent content for themselves. In short, these devices may replace our television "sets" (or perhaps the computer screen, the laptop, the cell phone have already replaced these sets), but the fundamental structures of television programs will likely remain for some time.

WORLDS WITHIN WORLDS

Once Upon a Time, like *Westworld*, deals in virtual reality. The difference in this case is that *Once*'s storyworld spaces spring from oral and text based narrative, fairy tales and nursery rhymes. In fact, all of these stories have been contained in a single book, a book with the title *Once Upon a Time*. If *Westworld* represents a possible future narrative storyworld, *Once Upon a Time* says something about the storyworlds of the past.

And yet like *Westworld*, *Once* isn't actually a storyworld from the past. It draws on those storyworlds for content, but it actually appears as a television storyworld. The show isn't, perhaps, the most innovative series in terms of its filmic techniques; it isn't especially realistic as a virtual reality. In fact, many of its special effects seem almost deliberately unrealistic. But there is something important about this show: its relationship to storytelling itself. *Once Upon a Time* is a show about fairy tales, a story about stories.

Once offers a perfect illustration of Bolter and Grusin's "remediation": it relies on the content of fairy tales and legends, old and new—*Snow White and the Seven Dwarves*, *Cinderella*, *The Little Mermaid*—repurposing these tales for a new medium, the medium of television. As a result the show highlights the important elements of television. It reworks these stories, for instance, because it simply can't end them. The traditional story of Rumpelstiltskin has a neat beginning, middle, and end, as traditional stories do. In contrast, the Rumpelstiltskin as imagined in *Once* moves fluidly in and out of many stories. We discover, for example, that his father is Peter Pan; he plays the role of the "Beast" to Belle's "beauty"; he is in some way connected to essentially every character's story, from Pinocchio to the Wicked Witch of the West. He is defined by the medium itself, the demands of serial storytelling that his tale remain open-ended. At the same time, the show plays on immediacy for many of its effects, relying on relationships between magical realms and the "realism" of Storybrooke. It is the contrast between the fantasy and the real that drives the show's tension.

In the end, *Once* serves as the ideal metaphor for all of television. It knows that storyworlds, virtual realities, have been around for as long as we have. It doesn't try to insist it invented the story. But in its format, the way these stories are relocated to a new world, the way in which the "reality" of this world interacts with the fairy tale worlds of Oz, Neverland, Wonderland, it enacts for us multiple levels of narrative realities. It isn't one world but many. Most importantly, *Once* works from within to create its stories. Henry is not merely a character in the series; he is the "author" of the "book," the writer of the tales that make up this reality. He both is the story and creates the story. In the end, this is what television offers us: a world that is self-aware, a world that knows its own power, a world large enough to explore indefinitely, where the stories knit themselves together, undo one another, and begin again, episode after episode, week after week.

NOTES

1. In fact, *Doctor Who* seems to be the first instance of television's mention of virtual reality, in a 1976 series, "The Deadly Assassin." Of course, it is also worth remembering that *Star Trek: the Next Generation* developed this technology in the form of the holodeck. For the most part, however, these examples—while significant—were fairly isolated in their time periods. I would argue that the more recent examples represent a kind of fixation on these technologies.

2. We have seen the VR trope in film as well—see *The Truman Show*, or *The Matrix, Wall-E*—and for that matter *Westworld* itself is based on Michael Chrichton's 1973 film of the same name.

Bibliography

"Active Virtual Reality for the Commercial Market." *Virtuix*. Accessed August 11, 2017. http:// http://www.virtuix.com/.

Allrath, Gaby and Marion Gymnich. 2005. *Narrative Strategies in Television Series*. London: Palgrave.

Amazing World of Doctor Who, The. 1976. London: BBC.

"American Academy of Pediatrics Announces New Recommendations for Children's Media Use." *American Academy of Pediatrics* website. Accessed August 11, 2017. https://www.aap.org/en-us/about-the-aap/aap-press-room/pages/american-academy-of-pediatrics-announces-new-recommendations-for-childrens-media-use.aspx.

Aristotle. *Poetics*. 1996. Translated by Malcolm Heath. New York: Penguin.

Bakhtin, Mikhail. 1981. "Epic and Novel." *The Dialogic Imagination*, 3–40. Austin: University of Texas Press.

Basulto, Dominic. "Why Google's New Quantum Computer Could Launch an Artificial Intelligence Arms Race." *The Washington Post*. December 10, 2015. https://www.washingtonpost.com/news/innovations/wp/2015/12/10/why-googles-new-quantum-computer-could-launch-an-artificial-intelligence-arms-race/?utm_term=.b2825e115a11.

Baudrillard, Jean. *Screened Out*. 2002. New York: Verso Books.

———. *Simulacra and Simulation*. 1994. Ann Arbor: University of Michigan Press.

Bianculli, David. 1992. *Teleliteracy*. New York: Continuum.

Bolter, Jay David and Richard Grusin. 2000. *Remediation*. Boston: MIT Press.

Booker, Keith. 1994. *The Dystopian Impulse in Modern Literature*. Westport, CT: Praeger.

Buckland, Warren. 2007. *The Cognitive Semiotics of Film*. Cambridge University Press.

———. "Orientation in Film Space: A Cognitive Semiotic Approach." *Recherches en Communication* 19 (2003): 87–102.

Burger, Allisa, ed. 2011. *The Television World of Pushing Daisies*. Jefferson, NC: McFarland.

Callaway, Ewen. "'Minimal' Cell Raises Stakes in Race to Harness Synthetic Life." *Nature*, March 24, 2016. https://www.nature.com/news/minimal-cell-raises-stakes-in-race-to-harness-synthetic-life-1.19633.

Canfield, David. "*Major Crimes* Creator Reveals Why Sharon Needed to Die." *Entertainment Weekly*, January 09, 2018. http://ew.com/tv/2018/01/09/major-crimes-series-finale-interview/.

Cervantes. 2005. *Don Quixote*. Translated by Edith Grossman. New York: Harper Perennial.

Corner, John. 1999. *Critical Ideas in Television Stories*. Oxford: Clarendon Press.

Cubitt, Sean. 2005. *The Cinema Effect*. Boston: MIT Press.

Curry, Nancy E. 1996. "The Reality of Make-Believe." In *Mr. Rogers' Neighborhood: Children, Television, and Fred Rogers*. Edited by Mark Collins and Margaret Mary Kimmel. Pittsburg: University of Pittsburg Press.

"Definitions of Science Fiction." *The Encyclopedia of Science Fiction*. Accessed August 11, 2017. http://www.sf-encyclopedia.com/entry/definitions_of_sf.

Devlin, Kate. "Rat's 'Brain' Used to Power Robot." *The Telegraph*. Accessed on August 13, 2008. https://www.telegraph.co.uk/news/2552973/Rats-brain-used-to-power-robot.html.

Duchan, Judith F., Gail A. Bruder, and Lynne E. Hewitt. 1994. "Prologue: A Simple Exercise in Narrative Understanding." *Deixis in Narrative*. Edited by Judith F. Duchan, Gail A. Bruder, and Lynne E. Hewitt, xvii-xvi. New York: Routledge.

Edgar, James. "'Captain Cyborg': The Man Behind the Controversial Turing Test Claims." *The Telegraph*, June 10, 2014. https://www.telegraph.co.uk/news/science/science-news/10888828/Captain-Cyborg-the-man-behind-the-controversial-Turing-Test-claims.html.

Ellis, John. 1992. *Visible Fictions*. New York: Routledge.

Fiedler, Leslie Fiedler. "The New Mutants." *Partisan Review* 32, no. 4 (Fall 1965), 505–525.

Flaubert, Gustave. 1904. *The Works of Gustave Flaubert in One Volume*. New York: Walter.

Friedman, Ted. 1995. "Making Sense of Software: Computer Games and Interactive Textuality." In *Cybersociety: Computer-Mediated Communication and Community*. Edited by Steven G. Jones, 78–39. Thousand Oaks, CA: Sage Publications.

Galbraith, Mary. 1994. "Decitic Shifty Theory and the Poetics of Involvement in Narrative." *Deixis in Narrative*. Edited by Judith F. Duchan, Gail A. Bruder, and Lynne E. Hewitt, 19–60. New York: Routledge.

Gerbner, George. 1996. "Fred Rogers and the Significance of Story." In *Mr. Rogers' Neighborhood: Children, Television, and Fred Rogers*. Edited by Mark Collins and Margaret Mary Kimmel. Pittsburg: University of Pittsburg Press.

Gerrig, Richard. 1999. *Experiencing Narrative Worlds*. Boulder: Westview Press.

Gerrold, David. 1974. *The World of Star Trek*. New York: Ballantine.

Glennon, Morgan. "The Messy World of *Justified*'s Women." *Huffington Post*. Last updated April 15, 2013. https://www.huffingtonpost.com/morgan-glennon/justified-fx_b_2674263.html.

Gray, Jonathan and Amanda D. Lotz. 2012. *Television Studies*. Malden, MA: Polity Press.

Hallin, Daniel C. 1989. *The Uncensored War: The Media and Vietnam*. Oakland: University of California Press.

Heath, Stephen and Gillian Skirrow. "Television: a World in Action." *Screen* 18, no. 2 (July 1977): 7–60.

Heim, Michael. 1994. *The Metaphysics of Virtual Reality*. Oxford: Oxford University Press.

Herman, David. 2004. *Story Logic: Problems and Possibilities of Narrative*. Lincoln: University of Nebraska Press.

Herzog, Werner, Director. 2011. *The Cave of Forgotten Dreams*. Doc Club.

Hibberd, James. "*The Sopranos* creator: A Prequel Might Work." *Entertainment Weekly*, June 14, 2017. http://ew.com/tv/2017/06/14/the-sopranos-prequel/.

Hoerner, Keisha L. "The Forgotten Battles: Congressional Hearings on Television Violence in the 1950s." *Web Journal of Mass Communication Research* 2, no. 3 (June 1999), n.p.

Hooten, Christopher. "*Lost* Writer Admits They Just Made It Up as They Went Along." *Independent*, January14, 2015. https://www.independent.co.uk/arts-entertainment/tv/news/lost-writer-admits-they-just-made-it-up-as-they-went-along-9977472.html.

Huxley, Aldous. 2004. *Brave New World*. New York: Harper Perennial.

Intintoli, Michael James. 1984. *Taking Soaps Seriously: The World of Guiding Light*. Santa Barbara: Praeger.

Ivakhiv, Adrian J. 2013. *Ecologies of the Moving Image*. Waterloo, ON: Wilfrid Laurier University Press.

Jacobs, Jason and Steven Peacock. 2013. Introduction in *Television Aesthetics and Style*. Edited by Jason Jacobs and Steven Peacock. New York: Bloomsbury Academic.

Jenkins, Henry. 2009. *Convergence Culture*. New York: New York University Press.

Johnson, Mark. 1990. *The Body in the Mind: The Bodily Basis of Meaning, Imagination, and Reason*. Chicago: University of Chicago Press.

Keefe, Patrick Radden. "The Uncannily Accurate Depiction of the Meth Trade in *Breaking Bad. The New Yorker*, July 13, 2012. https://www.newyorker.com/culture/culture-desk/the-uncannily-accurate-depiction-of-the-meth-trade-in-breaking-bad.

Kosnik, Abigail De. 2013. "One Life to Live: Soap Opera Storytelling." In *How to Watch Television*. Edited by Jason Mittell and Ethan Thompson. New York: New York University Press.

Kracauer, Siegfried. 1968. *Theory of Film: The Redemption of Physical Reality*. Oxford: Oxford University Press.

Lakoff, George. 2008. *Women, Fire and Dangerous Things*. Chicago: University of Chicago Press.

Leonard, Kendra Preston, editor. 2010. *Buffy, Ballads, and Bad Guys Who Sing: Music in the Worlds of Joss Whedon*. Lanham, Maryland: Scarecrow Press.

Lewis, David. "Truth in Fiction." *American Philosophical Quarterly* 15, no. 1. (Jan. 1978), 37–46.

Locke, John. 1690. "Of the State of Nature." In *Second Treatise on Government.*

Lushkov, Ayelet Haimson. 2017. *You Win or You Die: The Ancient World of* Game of Thrones. New York: I.B. Tauris.

MacRury, Ian and Michael Rustin. 2013. *The Inner World of* Doctor Who: *Psychoanalytic Reflections in Time and Space*. New York: Routledge.

Marr, Lisa Marr. 2015. Appendix. *Refiguring Minds in Narrative Media*, by David Ciccoricco, 241–248. Lincoln: University of Nebraska Press.

McDonnel, Mary. "Mary McDonnel on 'Major Crimes' Finale: 'I've Never Experienced Anything Quite Like This.'" *Variety*, January 15, 2018. http://variety.com/2018/tv/columns/mary-mcdonnell-major-crimes-finale-column-1202664536/.

McGonigal, Jane. 2011. *Reality is Broken*. London: Penguin Books.

McLuhan Marshall. 1964. *Understanding Media*. New York: McGraw-Hill.

Miller, Gerri. "Are Mermaids Real?" *Mother Nature Network*, May 24, 2013. https://www.mnn.com/lifestyle/arts-culture/stories/are-mermaids-real.

Miller, J. Hillis. 1995. *Topographies*. Stanford: Stanford University Press.

Minnow, Newton. "Television and the Public Interest." *Federal Communications Law Journal* 55, no. 3 (2003): 398.

Mittell, Jason. 2015. *Complex TV*. New York: New York University Press.

———. 2013. "The Qualities of Complexity: Vast Versus Dense Seriality in Contemporary Television." In *Television Aesthetics and Style*. Edited by Jason Jacobs and Steven Peacock. New York: Bloomsbury Academic, 45–56.

Molloy, Tim. "*The Walking Dead* Showrunner Reveals How It Doesn't End." *The Wrap*, June 27, 2012. https://www.thewrap.com/walking-dead-show-runner-glen-mazzara-reveals-how-it-doesnt-end-45301/.

Moore, Trent. "The World of *Preacher* Is a Violent Place in White-Knuckle New Clip from AMC's Series" *SyFywire*, April 12, 2016. http://www.syfy.com/syfywire/world-preacher-violent-place-white-knuckle-new-clip-amcs-series.

Nilges, Mathias. 2010. "The Aesthetics of Destruction: Contemporary U.S. Cinema and TV Culture." In *Reframing 9/11*. Edited by Jeff Birkenstein, Anna Froula, and Karen Randell, 23–34. New York: Coninuum.

O'Brien, Geoffrey. 1995. *The Phantom Empire*. New York: W.W. Norton, 1995.

Parrinder, Patrick. 1981. *Science Fiction: It's Criticism and Teaching*. London: Routledge, Kegan, and Paul.

Placido, Dani D. "Netflix's *Mindhunter* is so Good, It Makes Me Physically Sick." *Forbes*. October 18, 2017. https://www.forbes.com/sites/danidiplacido/2017/10/18/netflixs-mindhunter-is-so-good-it-makes-me-feel-physically-sick/#3e5762903b36.

Plato. 1968. *The Republic*. Translated by Allen Bloom. New York: Basic Books.

Porter, Jon. "Meet the Minds behind Nintendo's Switch HD Rumble Tech." *Techradar*, February 7, 2017. https://www.techradar.com/news/meet-the-minds-behind-nintendo-switchs-hd-rumble-tech.

Rheingold, Howard. 1992. *Virtual Reality*. New York: Simon and Schuster.

Ryan, Marie-Laure. 2015. *Narrative as Virtual Reality 2*. Baltimore: Johns Hopkins University Press.

———. 2005. "Possible Worlds Theory." In *Routledge Encyclopedia of Narrative Theory*. Edited by David Herman, Manfred Jahn, and Marie-Laure Ryan, 446-450. London: Routledge.

Sconce, Jeffrey. 2004. "What if? Charting Television's New Textual Boundaries" In *Television After TV*. Edited by Lynn Spiegel and Jan Olssen, 93–112. Durham, NC: Duke University Press.

Segal, Erwin M. 1994. "A Cognitive-Phenomenological Theory of Fictional Narrative." In *Deixis in Narrative*. Edited by Judith F. Duchan, Gail A. Bruder, and Lynne E. Hewitt, 61–78. New York: Routledge.

———. 1994. "Narrative Comprehension and the Role of Deictic Shift Theory." In *Deixis in Narrative*. Edited by Judith F. Duchan, Gail A. Bruder, and Lynne E. Hewitt, 3–18. New York: Routledge.

Sepinwall, Alan. "*Battlestar Galactica*: Ronald D. Moore Finale Q&A." *NJ.com*, March 20, 2009. http://sepinwall.blogspot.com/2009/03/battlestar-galactica-ronald-d-moore.html.

Speer, Nicole K, Jeremy R. Reynolds, Kheena M. Swallow, and Jeffrey M. Zacks. "Reading Stories Activates Neural Representations of Perceptual and Motor Experiences." *Psychological Science* 20 (2009), 989–999.

Surette, Tim. "*Revolution* Series Finale Review: Keeping the Lights On for No Reason at All." *TV.com*, May 22, 2014. http://www.tv.com/news/revolution-series-finale-review-keeping-the-lights-on-for-no-reason-at-all-140070065880/.

Suvin, Darko. 2016. *Metamorphoses of Science Fiction: On the Poetics and History of a Literary Genre*. New York: Peter Lang Publishers.

Tallerico, Bryan. "Watch the Real-Life Interviews with Serial Killer Edmund Kemper." *Vulture.com*, October 18, 2017. http://www.vulture.com/2017/10/mindhunter-who-is-ed-kemper-serial-killer.html.

Vint, Sherryl. 2013. *The Wire*. Detroit: Wayne State University Press.

Wallis, John and James Aston. "Doomsday America: The Pessimistic Turn of Post-9/11 Apocalyptic Cinema." *Journal of Religion and Popular Culture* 23, no 1 (2011), 53–64.

Walton, Kendall. 1993. *Mimesis as Make-Believe: On the Foundations of the Representational Arts*. Boston: Harvard University Press.

Williams, Raymond. 2003. *Television: Technology and Cultural Form*. New York: Routledge.

Winnicott, D. W. 2005. *Playing and Reality*. London: Routledge.

Wolff, Michael. 2015. *Television Is the New Television*. New York: Portfolio.

Wyndham, John. 2003. *The Day of the Triffids*. New York: Penguin.

List of TV Shows Referenced

3rd Rock from the Sun (1996–2001)
19 Kids and Counting (2008–)
24 (2001–2010)
30 Rock (2006–2013)
All in the Family (1971–1979)
American Family, An (1973)
American Idol (2002–)
Arthur (1996–)
Bachelor, The (2002–)
Barney and Friends (1992–2009)
Bates Motel (2013–2017)
Batman (1966–1968)
Battlestar Galactica (2004–2009)
Beverly Hillbillies, The (1962–1971)
Big Brother (2000–)
Blue's Clues (1996–2007)
Bob Newhart Show, The (1972–1978)
Bob the Builder (1999–)
Breaking Bad (2008–2013)
Broadchurch (2013–2017)
Buffy the Vampire Slayer (1992)
Buffy the Vampire Slayer (1997–2003)
Caprica (2009–2010)
Captain Kangaroo (1955–1992)
Cheers (1982–1993)
Closer, The (2005–2012)
Community (2009–2015)

Coronation Street (1960–)
Dexter (2006–2013)
Dick Van Dyke Show, The (1961–1966)
Disney's Wonderful World of Color (1954–1991)
Doctor Who (1963–)
Dog Whisperer, The (2004–2016)
Dollhouse (2009–2010)
Doogie Howser, M.D. (1989–1993)
Dora the Explorer (2005–2015)
Eureka (2006–2012)
Family Guy (1998–)
Fargo (2014–)
Father Knows Best (1954–1960)
Fear the Walking Dead (2015–)
Flashforward (2009–2010)
Flintstones, The (1960–1966)
Fraggle Rock (1983–1987)
Game of Thrones (2011–)
General Hospital (1963–)
Gilligan's Island (1964–1967)
Gilmore Girls (2000–2007)
Girls (2012–2017)
Green Acres (1965–1971)
Gunsmoke (1955–1975)
Happy Days (1974–1984)
Haven (2010–2015)
Hill Street Blues (1981–1987)
Home Improvement (1991–1999)
Homeland (2011–)
Honeymooners, The (1955–1956)
House of Cards (2013–)
Howdy Doody Show, The (1947–1960)
I Love Lucy (1951–1957)
Iron Chef (1993–1999)
It's Garry Shandling's Show (1986–1990)
Jericho (2006–2008)
Jetsons, The (1962–1963)
Jon and Kate Plus 8 (2007–)
Justified (2010–2015)
Killing, The (2011–2014)
L.A. Law (1986–1994)
Larry Sanders Show, The (1992–1998)

Last Ship, The (2014–)
Law and Order (1990–2010)
Law and Order: Special Victims Unit (1999–)
Lazytown (2004–2014)
Leave It to Beaver (1957–1963)
Legion (2017–)
Life on Mars (U.K.) (2006–2007)
Little People, Big World (2006–)
Lost (2004–2010)
Love Boat, The (1977–1987)
Mad Men (2007–2015)
Major Crimes (2012–2018)
Man in the High Castle, The (2015–)
Marvel's Agents of S.H.I.E.L.D. (2015–)
Mary Tyler Moore Show, The (1970–1977)
*M*A*S*H* (1972–1983)
Mermaids: New Evidence (2013)
Mermaids: The Body Found (2011)
Monster Squid: the Giant is Real (2013)
Mork and Mindy (1978–1982)
Mr. Robot (2015–)
Mr. Rogers' Neighborhood (1968–2001)
Newhart (1982–1990)
NYPD Blue (1993–2005)
Office, The (U.S.) (2005–2013)
Once Upon a Time (2011–)
Orphan Black (2013–2017)
Pee Wee's Playhouse (1986–1991)
Perry Mason (1957–1966)
Postcards from Buster (2004–2012)
Preacher (2016–)
Psych (2006–2014)
Psycho (1960)
Quantum Leap (1989–1993)
Revolution (2012–2014)
Rockford Files, The (1974–1980)
Route 66 (1960–1964)
Sesame Street (1969–)
Seinfeld (1989–1998)
Sherlock (2010–)
Sopranos, The (1999–2007)
South Park (1997–)

Spongebob Squarepants (1999–)
Star Trek (1966–1969)
St. Elsewhere (1982–1988)
Stranger Things (2016–)
Superior Donuts (2017–)
Survivor (2000–)
Teletubbies (1997–2001)
Thomas and Friends (1984–)
True Blood (2008–2014)
Twilight Zone, The (1959–1964)
Twin Peaks (1990–1991)
Under the Dome (2013–2015)
Walking Dead, The (2010–)
Wayward Pines (2015–2016)
West Wing, The (1999–2006)
Westworld (2016–)
Wire, The (2002–2008)
X-Files, The (1993–)

Index

About the Author

M. King Adkins received his PhD in English from the University of Georgia in 2007 and completed a post-doctoral fellowship at Georgia Tech in 2011. Currently, he serves as associate professor at the South Dakota School of Mines and Technology, where he teaches courses in literature, popular culture, and writing, and pursues collaborative projects between humanities and computer science. His previous work includes *New Wave: Image is Everything*, which explores intersections between 1980s music, culture, and postmodern theory.

www.ingramcontent.com/pod-product-compliance
Ingram Content Group UK Ltd.
Pitfield, Milton Keynes, MK11 3LW, UK
UKHW020209290926
15470UKWH00001B/78

9 781498 529600